Mosques of Istanbul

Mosques of Istanbul

Including the Mosques of Bursa and Edirne

Henry Matthews

SCALA

CONTENTS

AUTHOR'S NOTE

I am deeply indebted to the late Aptullah Kuran, whose writings on Ottoman architecture offered me inspiration and a wealth of knowledge. Without his years of scholarship, this book would not have been possible. I appreciate his permission to reproduce several of his drawings. His death in April 2002 was a great loss to those who knew him and admired his work. I thank Reha Günay for allowing me to include some of his photographs; I value his friendship and advice. I warmly acknowledge the information and insights I received from the books and articles of Alpaslan Ataman, Jale Erzen, John Freely, Godfrey Goodwin and Doğan Kuban, and I am grateful to Caroline Finkel who read part of my manuscript and gave me essential help on Ottoman history. I thank Selim Kuru for translating Tursun Beg's description of Mehmet II's first visit to Hagia Sophia. I acknowledge the outstanding scholarship of Gülru Necipoğlu, whose book *The Age of Sinan: Architectural Culture in the Ottoman Empire* will be the definitive work on the great sixteenth-century architect. Since it was published shortly before this book went to press, I was able to make some last minute corrections for which I am indebted to the author. These include a major revision of dates (see note below). I thank Brian Johnson, who originally helped me to conceive this book and who gave me essential advice. I also thank my wife Susan Platt, who, as a Fulbright Fellow teaching art history and theory in Istanbul, encouraged me to spend almost a year there. Her support, wisdom and patience helped to sustain this project.

Note on the dates and names of mosques

The mosques in this book were arranged in chronological order according to the dates established by Aptullah Kuran and others. Prior to publication, I altered the dates of several mosques by Mimar Sinan to reflect recent research by Gülru Necipoğlu. As a result, in a few cases, the mosques illustrated are not exactly in chronological order.

In the numbered heading for each mosque, I use the correct Turkish name (for example, Süleymaniye Camii) but in the text itself I refer to them as mosques.

I use the name Hagia Sophia to describe the building when it was a Byzantine church; when I refer to it after the conquest, I use the Ottoman name Aya Sofya.

Note on the Glossary

Words included in the Glossary at the back of this book have been italicised in the text for easy reference.

Henry Matthews, 2009

FOREWORD

Mosques dominate the silhouette of Istanbul. After the Turkish conquest, the city's character changed with the building of mosques, which rose high above the skyline, challenging the monuments of earlier centuries. Built in impressive *külliyes* (complexes of educational and charitable buildings), they offer unique examples of the progress of Ottoman architecture, which occupies an important place in Islamic and indeed world architecture.

Ottoman architecture emerged towards the end of the fourteenth century and acquired its distinctive character by the beginning of the fifteenth century. The best architectural examples of this period are the mosques of Bursa. As Ottoman architecture developed, tile decoration began to play a greater role, and the city of İznik became the centre of tile production. At first, tiles were used only to embellish the *mihrab* in mosques; later, they often covered the walls.

Ottoman mosque architecture made a significant leap in the design of the central dome. The best example of this development is Istanbul's Beyazit II Mosque, built at the beginning of the sixteenth century. Fifty years later, Ottoman architecture reached its zenith with the architect Sinan, who constructed about 400 buildings, with more than 80 of these being large mosques, and the rest consisting of small mosques, medreses, tombs, bridges, soup kitchens (*imarets*), caravanserais, hospitals, baths, palaces and aqueducts.

Sinan's influence continued up to the middle of the eighteenth century, when Ottoman architecture came under the influence of Baroque architecture. The mosques of Istanbul built in the nineteenth century display the influence of European Neoclassicism.

This book traces the evolution of Ottoman mosque architecture in Istanbul, Bursa and Edirne, from its origins almost to the present. First planned as a guidebook specifically for foreigners, it was decided to translate it for Turkish readers too since there is no similar work in the Turkish market of the same content and volume.

The progress of Ottoman architecture, its central place in the development of Ottoman civilisation, and the richness of its tradition are covered in the 49 examples of mosques described in this book. Abundant illustrations, ground plans, a comprehensive index and copious supplementary material make this volume an important reference work as much as a guidebook. It is an invaluable resource both for travellers who have the opportunity to visit the mosques of Istanbul, as well as for those who simply wish to learn more about this fascinating aspect of Turkish history and culture.

Though the author of *Mosques of Istanbul* is from a different cultural and religious background, he has treated this central topic of Turkish-Islamic culture with sensitivity and scholarly understanding that is worthy of praise. Hopefully, this insightful and informative book will pave the way for more works of a similar kind.

Dr M. Numan Malkoç
Editor of *İstanbul'un Camileri* (the Turkish edition of *Mosques of Istanbul*)

INTRODUCTION

If you were to look south across the Golden Horn from the high vantage point of Galata Tower, you would see, on the undulating ridge beyond, a series of vast domes and minarets. It might be assumed that the rather similar mosques on the skyline are of the same basic design with a few minor changes. Further exploration would soon reveal, however, that the religious architecture of the Ottoman Empire went through a series of transformations. This book aims to show that the mosques you see before you represent many stages in the evolution of a remarkable building type. It introduces architects who experimented boldly with structure, space and light, and explains the principles that made their designs possible. You will witness the brilliance of Michelangelo's contemporary, Mimar Sinan, who experimented with the design of large domes for 50 years and achieved dazzling innovations. In the nearby cities of Bursa and Edirne, you will encounter further chapters in the story of Ottoman mosques, revealing both the early stages of their development and one of the peaks of Mimar Sinan's architectural creation.

The construction of imperial mosques and their associated buildings was fundamental to the planning and growth of Istanbul. The mosques were not simply isolated monuments. They were part of complexes known as *külliyes*, which included schools, hospitals, kitchens to feed students and the poor, baths, and accommodation for travellers. Thus the mosques were instruments of enlightened social policy in the city. Clean water flowed from their fountains and they offered peaceful gardens for repose. A fascinating aspect of these buildings is the light they shed on the patronage of the *sultans*, the *viziers*, and, not least, the *valide sultans*. As the mothers of sultans, some of these women exercised enormous political power and demonstrated their status in the mosques that they commissioned. The building of mosques proclaimed the greatness and piety of the sultans as well as the wealth and influence of other patrons.

If your reverie on Galata Tower coincides with the call to prayer, you will hear the sound of the *müezzins* of all the mosques joining together in their exhortation to the faithful. As their voices rise and fall, merging with each other or standing out distinctly, you will be witnessing a powerful manifestation of the world's second most popular religion. Even in the secular state of Turkey, the mosque and its rituals is central to many people's lives. A visit to Turkey, rich as it is in remains of ancient civilisations and phenomena of modern life, would be incomplete without an exploration of Ottoman mosques.

From the Galata Tower, looking south across the water at the long ridge covered by the Ottoman city, you can see the distinctive outline of Topkapı Palace to the left, at the tip of the peninsula, above the point where the Golden Horn flows into the Bosphorus. Beyond it, in the distance, lies the Sea of Marmara. Further to the left, looking east, is the Asian side of Istanbul and the Bosphorus flowing by. A little to the right of Topkapı is the powerful form of Aya Sofya, the Byzantine church built by the Emperor Justinian in 537 CE. The huge arches and massive buttresses that hold up the dome can easily be made out from the Galata Tower. Four minarets, added after it became a mosque, surround it. Just to the left of Aya Sofya is Hagia Eireni. This church, erected in the early sixth century, is a forerunner to Aya Sofya. To the right are the dome and six minarets of the grandiose Sultan Ahmet Camii (1609–16), built in the Late Classical era. Continuing in the same westerly direction is the Baroque mosque,

Nuruosmaniye Camii. Almost directly below it on the water, to the left of the Galata Bridge, is the Late Classical Yeni Valide Camii with its many small domes clustered around the central one. Next on the skyline is Sultan Beyazit II Camii (c.1500–06), built with a dome and two half domes in the manner of Aya Sofya. Set back a little from the waterfront, just below the tall tower to the right of Beyazit II Camii, you should be able to find among the commercial buildings the dome of Rüstem Paşa Camii. Its tiled interior is one of the sixteenth-century architect Mimar Sinan's most appealing spaces. Above and further to the right is Sinan's great masterpiece, built on a broad terrace and dominating the city. This is Süleymaniye Camii (1550–57), built by Süleyman the Magnificent. Its four minarets of two different heights give it a distinctive silhouette. Its *külliye* covers many acres and you will be able to perceive its orderly form in a line of miniature domes. Şehzade Camii (1543–48) is the next to the right. This was designed by Sinan for Süleyman to commemorate his son, who died tragically at the age of 21. It was the first mosque with a central dome and four half domes, a pattern to be followed often in the future. Moving further along the skyline, the eighteenth-century Fatih Camii stands above the Atatürk Bridge. This replaced the mosque built by Mehmet II (known as Fatih, meaning "conqueror"), destroyed by an earthquake in 1766. At the near end of the bridge is Azapkapı Camii, another of Sinan's works. The last mosques that are easily visible on the ridge are Sultan Selim Camii, built by Süleyman to honour his father, Selim I, and Mihrimah Sultan Camii at Edirnekapı, a gate in the Land Walls. Further west at the head of the Golden Horn lies the important pilgrimage site of Eyüp with its two mosques.

The short introductory chapters of this book include a brief history of the Islamic religion and an introduction to Muslim beliefs and practices. The evolution from the early mosques, built without domes in North Africa and the Middle East, to the high-domed mosques for which Turkey is famous, is explored, and descriptions of the various mosques are arranged chronologically to highlight this evolution. Although the book focuses on Istanbul, mosques in the nearby cities of Bursa and Edirne are also included. Both cities possess important early mosques of a type not found in Istanbul. Furthermore, Edirne also boasts Mimar Sinan's finest achievement. Having seen the Şehzade and Süleymaniye mosques of Istanbul, a tour of Selimiye Camii in Edirne completes a story of structural daring and design virtuosity.

The choice of mosques is my own, and reflects my interests. They were selected for their historical interest, architectural merit, and to represent all the main stylistic periods. Two Byzantine churches are also included because of their strong influence on Ottoman mosques, plus one other because it highlights the different needs of church and mosque. Tombs and other buildings associated with the mosques are not described in detail. A few subsidiary buildings that are open to the public are mentioned. Stained glass windows are not covered, as not much original glass remains. This is because the glass was set mainly in plaster tracery rather than stone, and the plaster subsequently deteriorated. In the 49 mosques explored here, there is more to see than can possibly be described in one book. It would be tedious to read about 49 *mihrabs*, 49 *minbers* and countless *sebils*, while information on the calligraphic inscriptions alone could fill a large volume. Instead, I have concentrated most of all on the spatial qualities and structural systems of the mosques.

THE ISLAMIC RELIGION

Muhammad ibn Abdallah (570–632), a merchant of the city of Mecca in present-day Saudi Arabia, lived in troubled times. Arab tribes were fighting relentlessly against each other, and their polytheistic religion offered no solutions to the breakdown of their society. They worshipped many gods and lacked scriptures and moral teachings like those of the Jews and the Christians. Muhammad's own tribe, the Quraysh (keepers of a holy shrine, called the Ka'ba, at Mecca), was growing rich on trade, but He was outraged by the greed of the wealthy and their lack of concern for the suffering of the poor and weak. Every year in the month of Ramadan He would retreat to a cave in a nearby mountain to meditate in private. In the year 610 He awoke there in the night and, under the power of an unseen force, began to speak the first words of what was to become the *Qur'an*. In fear, He confided in His wife Khadija and her Christian cousin, who immediately saw similarities to the revelations received from God by Moses and Jesus. The revelations continued, always accompanied by a sense of submission to a higher power; Muhammad knew that they came from Allah (the name of God in Arabic). His wife, a wealthy businesswoman who had been His employer, was immensely supportive to Him as He tried to understand where His duty lay. He eventually became convinced that he had been chosen as a Prophet of God, and began to preach and make converts. The new religion appealed to the poor, for the Prophet Muhammad, peace be upon Him, taught that wealth should be shared with the less fortunate. Many women, slaves and the very poor joined Him, and before long 70 families counted themselves as Muslims. However, the affluent leaders of Mecca felt threatened by His message and placed a ban on trade or marriage with them. During the period of deprivation that followed, the Prophet Muhammad's beloved wife Khadija died.

In 620, a delegation of people came to Him from Yathrib, 250 miles north of Mecca. They converted to Islam, and persuaded the Muslims to leave Mecca and settle in their city. This emigration to Yathrib is called "hijra". The city became known as Medinat al-Nabi (City of the Prophet), or Medina for short. For the first time in the Arab world, religion became a stronger bond than the tribe. The pronouncements that the Prophet Muhammad received throughout His life, and passed on to His followers, represented a code of human behaviour with peace and social justice at its core, as well as instruction on how Allah, the one God, should be worshipped. "Islam" means "surrendering"; it calls on Muslims who profess Islam to submit to the will of God and to follow His laws. At Medina the first mosque was built, consisting of a simple shelter on one side of a courtyard, with its roof held up by palm trunks. The Prophet Muhammad established the orientation of prayer towards Mecca and marked the *qibla* wall that faced in that direction with a stone. He preached standing on a tree trunk.

The Quraysh were angered by His success, and vowed to destroy Islam. After several years of fighting between the Muslims and the Meccans, the Prophet Muhammad made a courageous move. He went with a thousand unarmed followers to the Ka'ba at Mecca for the annual pilgrimage known as the "hajj". Since weapons were forbidden in this holy place, no harm came to them and He was able to make a peace treaty. Following this amazing event, conversion to Islam increased rapidly. When the Meccans violated the treaty He returned to their city with ten thousand followers. Seeing the overwhelming numbers the Meccans surrendered, and He was able to take the city without bloodshed. Islam had prevailed. He destroyed the idols around the Ka'ba, and established it as the sanctuary of the one God Allah. Many of His opponents converted to Islam, and the Arabs abandoned tribal warfare to rally to the cause of a unifying religion. After the Prophet Muhammad's death the Islamic community spread out of the Arabian peninsula, and His successors carried the banner of Islam to the Mediterranean shores of North Africa and the steppes of Central Asia.

Like most people in His time the Prophet Muhammad was illiterate, but His revelations, accepted as the word of God, were memorised and written down under the leadership of His successors. In 653, during the reign of Osman, the third caliph, the canonical text of the *Qur'an* was established. This became the sole version on which the Islamic religion is founded. The nature of a good Muslim's duties is manifested in the "Five Pillars of Islam".

The Five Pillars of Islam

The essence of the religion is to be found in this series of duties to be observed by all Muslims.

Shahada. This is the profession of faith, and is expressed by the often-repeated words: "I bear witness that there is no god but God and I bear witness that the Prophet Muhammad is the messenger of God." The *müezzins* broadcast these words from minarets during the call to prayer. They can also be seen in beautiful calligraphy on the walls of mosques. Shahada represents the essential core of the Islamic faith – submission to God and acknowledgment that Muhammad is His Prophet.

Salat. This ritual prayer is performed five times a day. Evidence of this duty can be seen in every mosque at prayer times, but particularly around midday on Fridays. Before prayer, Muslims must purify themselves by washing their faces, mouths, hands and feet. Fountains for ablutions (often beautiful works of art) are provided at every mosque.

Shoes are removed and men often cover their heads while praying. Prayer must be conducted facing in the direction of the Ka'ba in Mecca. Mosques are always oriented towards Mecca and the faithful arrange themselves in rows parallel to the *qibla* wall, the wall facing in that direction. Whether praying alone or with their community at prayer times, they recite a set of verses from the *Qur'an* while going through a series of postures, progressing from an upright position with the hands facing forwards just behind the ears, to a completely prostrate position with the forehead touching the prayer mat. During prayers in the mosque the *imam* in his role as prayer leader coordinates the movements of all, but between official times you will see individuals performing the same ritual alone.

Zakat. The prescribed giving of alms to the poor and needy, this involves giving away a certain portion of one's wealth in charity. The endowment of *külliyes* (religious complexes) by sultans and important officials is an example of Zakat on a

grand scale. They included such institutions as hospitals and soup kitchens to feed the poor.

Sawm. This is the fasting during daylight hours in Ramadan, the ninth month of the Islamic calendar. Smoking and sex are also proscribed between sunrise and sunset. Near many mosques you will see people gathering at sunset during Ramadan to eat a communal meal. Children, the old, the sick, and pregnant women are exempted from fasting.

Hajj. The pilgrimage to Mecca in Saudi Arabia is the duty of every Muslim, except those too poor or too sick to make the journey. It must be done at a specific time of year, between the first and the tenth day of Dhu al-hijja (the month of pilgrimage in the Islamic calendar).

One important aspect of Islam is respect for Christians and Jews, who are considered "Ahl al-kitab" (People of the Book). According to Islamic belief, the Christian and Jewish scriptures, the Bible and the Torah, were revealed by God. Although thought to be incomplete, these books are seen to comprise the same substance as the *Qur'an*, which is considered to be the definitive version of God's message to humanity. Islam embodies many ideas of the Old Testament of the Bible. It adopts Adam and Eve, and the prophets Abraham, Moses, David and Solomon. While Muslims do not believe that Jesus Christ was the Son of God, they honour him as a prophet who came before the ultimate prophet, Muhammad. Although Islam was spread on a wave of conquest, populations were not forced to convert; Christians and Jews were permitted to practise their own religions. Indeed during the Ottoman Empire Christians and Jews, fleeing religious persecution in Europe, found a safe haven in Islamic countries, and particularly in Istanbul. An interesting and historically significant aspect of Islam was the interplay of faith and reason. While in the West the schism between science and religion held back advances in natural science, Islamic scholars, building on the philosophy and science of the Classical world, made great advances in philosophy, mathematics, anatomy, astronomy and other branches of science.

Islam also protects the status of women in society. Men and women are regarded as equal before God. Muslim women received rights of inheritance and divorce long before such rights were accepted in the West. The *Qur'an* demanded that women dress modestly.

The First Caliphs

After the death of the Prophet Muhammad in 632, His place as religious and temporal leader of the Islamic community was taken by His father-in-law and close friend Abu Bakr, who became the first caliph. "Khalifa" in Arabic, caliph has the meaning of "delegate", indicating that Abu Bakr did not rule on his own authority, but as a representative of God and His messenger. During his two-year reign he devoted himself to maintaining peace and unity among the tribes who followed the Prophet Muhammad. His successor, Omar, led his people to an astonishing victory against the Persians in 637, and thus brought the entire Persian Empire under their control. A year later they took Jerusalem and by 641 they ruled Syria, Palestine and Egypt. The third caliph, the Prophet Muhammad's son-in-law Osman, continued the conquests and acted as a moral leader to his people. However, in a few years dissent had erupted and Osman was murdered in 656. Another son-in-law and the Prophet's cousin Ali were attacked by some for not avenging Osman's death. Others revered Ali and believed that, as the Prophet Muhammad's closest relative, he should have been the first caliph. After the assassination of Ali, a deep division developed between those who wanted Ali's sons Hasan and Husein to rule and the supporters of Mu'awiya, founder of the Umayyad dynasty in Syria. The rift never healed. The majority of Muslims (including most of the Turkish people), known as the Sunnis, affirm the legitimacy of the caliphs who succeeded the Prophet Muhammad, as well as Mu'awiya and the ensuing Umayyad rulers. A minority, however, particularly in Persia, never accepted Mu'awiya, regarding Ali and his descendants as the rightful leaders

of the community. They are known as Shi'ites. The difference between Sunnis and Shi'ites was largely political at first, but doctrinal differences developed.

In many Ottoman mosques the names of the first four caliphs, along with those of Hasan and Husein, are displayed in beautiful calligraphy beside those of God and the Prophet Muhammad. For example, they appear in roundels in the pendentives of Rüstem Paşa Camii in Istanbul.

Sufism and Dervish Orders

Sufism emerged, particularly among Shi'ites, as a mystical tradition stressing the union of the soul with God. Sufi dervishes often lived an ascetic life, or engaged in ecstatic practices involving dance, music, poetry and singing. The so-called Whirling Dervishes are the best known in Turkey, but there were other orders. Not enclosed in monasteries or bound by vows, they differ greatly from Christian monks, and travelled from place to place to bring spiritual experience to the faithful. Travelling dervishes are significant to the study of Ottoman mosques, particularly before the mid-sixteenth century, as accommodation for them was often built next to the prayer halls.

Women in Mosques

Traditionally Turkish women were encouraged to pray at home or, if attending the mosque, to use the galleries or the areas reserved for them near the entrance, for the sake of propriety.

above left
Men performing their ablutions at a fountain in the garden of Atik Valide Sultan Camii in Üsküdar.

above right
An old man reading the *Qur'an* in the tomb of Yıldırım Beyazit Camii in Bursa.

VISITING MOSQUES

Visitors are welcomed into most Turkish mosques, but they should show respect by following a few simple rules:

Avoid visiting at prayer times, especially during noon prayers on Fridays. If you do so, stand quietly at the back, and refrain from talking or taking photographs.

Take off your shoes before entering. There are usually shelves inside where you can place them.

Make sure that your shoulders and knees are covered. Do not wear shorts.

Women should cover their heads. Larger mosques may have scarves to loan, but it is advisable always to carry one. Men should remove their hats.

Do not take photographs with flash. If you plan to photograph interiors, take fast film. In some mosques, special permission is required for photography.

Avoid disturbing worshippers in any way.

Prayer times vary according to the season. Times are generally posted in mosques and announced in newspapers and, if in doubt, you will be alerted by the *müezzin*'s call to prayer.

Opening Times

Most mosques are open all day, but some are only open at prayer times. The best way to visit these is to wait quietly in the porch or courtyard during the prayers, and enter after people have finished coming out. Sometimes when mosques are closed, you will be able to find a caretaker who can let you in. The mosques featured in this book are assumed to be open daily unless otherwise stated in the text. However, the situation may sometimes change.

opposite
Şehzade Camii: Interior view including the *mihrab* and the *minber*. The beautifully decorated *mihrab* on the left, with its stalactite vault rising to a sharp point, is in its usual position on the *qibla* wall. The *minber* is always located to the right of the *mihrab*.

Origins and principles

The followers of Muhammad had few needs in their places of worship. While the elaborate liturgy of the Christian Church required buildings for the celebration of mass, the Islamic place of prayer demanded no particular building shape or form. In Christian churches the apse or choir, for the priests and monks, is separated from the lay people's nave and transepts. With the altar at the east end as the focus of the service, provision is made for processions and other rituals. In the Islamic religion there are no priests. Apart from readings from the *Qur'an* and Friday sermons on moral, political and social issues, the sole activity in the mosque is prayer. This requires a space protected from sun and rain, where the faithful can pray individually or together in large numbers. The only other needs are the *mihrab*, a niche in the *qibla* wall on the side facing towards Mecca to which the prayers are directed, the *minber* or raised platform for the delivery of sermons, and a place for ablutions. This is either an elegant fountain (*şadırvan*) in the centre of the court, or less formally in a garden; or it might be a row of taps and benches along the wall of the mosque. In early Ottoman times the *şadırvan* was sometimes within the mosque. In addition, the minaret, from which the *müezzin* calls the faithful to prayer five times a day, became an essential element of the mosque from early times. At Friday prayers the many worshippers are expected to follow prayer leaders and move together in unison, so it was important for Ottoman architects to create a clear view across the space. As the design of mosques progressed under the Ottoman sultans, the architects succeeded in opening up the space and reducing the mass of the structural supports that obstructed vision.

An important consideration in the design of mosques is the prohibition on images representing humans or animals, as this is regarded as idolatrous. While Christian churches are ornamented with sculpture, painting and stained glass on religious themes, Islamic religious buildings are enriched only with abstract decoration and calligraphy. Devoid of the clutter of altars, holy relics, elaborate tombs, works of art, fonts, confessionals and pews, the interiors of mosques appear open and spacious. Surfaces are often enriched with decorative designs based on geometric patterns or plant forms, but the supreme ornament is in the form of calligraphic inscriptions, usually quoting from the *Qur'an*.

Süleymaniye Camii: The inscription on this ceramic plaque, in the courtyard of the mosque, reads: "In the name of God, the Merciful, the Compassionate; God, there is no god but He, the Living, the Everlasting."

Pre-Ottoman mosques

The first Muslims, coming from a nomadic life in Arabia, had few architectural traditions of their own, but the lands they conquered were rich in art and architecture. The sophistication of Greco-Roman cities that fell to Islamic warriors offered inspiration for a new architecture fulfilling religious and social needs. They adopted various Roman and Christian building types, and freely adapted them to serve their own purposes. The longitudinal basilica, leading towards the altar in the apse, had proved to be ideal for Christian worship, and for Islamic mosques similar aisled halls were built. Further aisles were sometimes added to make larger spaces. Columns from existing Roman buildings were often re-used. In Christian churches the long axis is almost always towards the altar, but it was usually turned 90 degrees in the early mosques so that the *mihrab* was on the short axis. Large courtyards were usually added, providing a peaceful transition from the city streets or the openness of the desert, as well as extra space for worshippers. To give shade, the courtyards were surrounded by arcades. An example of an early mosque is the one built at Kufa in Iraq in 637. Here a five-aisled hall stands on one side of a courtyard, with two rows of columns supporting a roof on the other sides. The concept is extremely simple. A broad expanse of horizontal space is interrupted only by slender columns. In Jerusalem, the Dome of the Rock (completed 691) was closely modelled after Early Christian martyrs' tombs. The dome covered the rock where, according to Muslim belief, the Prophet Muhammad ascended to heaven, so it served a unique purpose. Several centuries passed before the use of domes was common.

Ottoman Calligraphy

"To read beautiful calligraphy is like smelling the aroma of a tulip."
(Kazasker Mustafa Izzet Efendi)

Calligraphy is the most important art of Islam because it records and transmits the word of God. The many references in the *Qur'an* to writing include a description of the Almighty who "taught man with the pen". Not surprisingly then, calligraphers enjoyed a higher status than painters of miniatures or architects. The Ottoman sultans encouraged them to reach new heights by commissioning exquisite *Qur'ans*, elaborate documents for their libraries, and inscriptions to adorn their mosques. Calligraphers began to experiment with the expressive potential of the Arabic script, and developed new styles. Some sultans became calligraphers themselves. For example, Beyazit II, as crown prince and Governor of Amasya, studied the art under Sheikh Hamdullah ibn Mustafa Dede and, when he became sultan, invited him to Istanbul to oversee the office of calligraphy in the palace. In addition to numerous *Qur'ans* and *suras* (chapters of the *Qur'an*), this great master made the inscriptions in the *mihrab* and dome of Beyazit's imperial mosque.

The earliest style of calligraphy was the Kufic script that emerged in the time of Ali, the fourth caliph. This was the only form used for the *Qur'an* until the eleventh century. It was stiff and rectilinear, with rather thick strokes. In contrast, the later scripts flowed freely on the page, and calligraphers were able to add vitality by opposing strong verticals with diagonals and supple curves. A play between large and small letters was created, and diacritical marks became eloquent visual accents. Not limited to straight lines across the page, as was normal in the West,

calligraphers could create subtle interactions between the letters and the surfaces they occupied.

The six commonest scripts in Ottoman calligraphy are characterised by the thickness of the pens that were used, the proportions of the letters, and the balance between straight lines and curves. They also tended to serve different purposes. "Muhakkak" and "reyhanî" were well suited, respectively, to the transcription of large and small *Qur'ans*; "tevkî" and "rik'a" were used more for official documents. "Sülüs", sometimes combined with "nesih", offered the greatest scope for artistic expression. Its free-flowing curves and strong verticals were ideally suited to large architectural inscriptions. When letters are joined together in a continuous chain, the style is called "celî sülüs". This is the style, either in blue and white tiled panels or in gold leaf on carved stone, that usually adorns mosques. These were first executed with reed pens on parchment or paper and overlaid with a square grid of lines for transfer to tiles or directly to the wall. Some inscriptions were divided in two halves, one side being the mirror image of the other. This style can be seen in the large Kufic designs on the piers in the Ulucami at Bursa.

In Islamic mosques calligraphy takes the place of the sculpture and stained glass of Christian cathedrals. The diverse ways in which the names of God, the Prophet Muhammad, and the first caliphs are written is quite remarkable. For example, in Rüstem Paşa Camii the vivacious opposition of large and small letters is quite different from the rectilinear geometry in Şehzade Camii. The roundels in Süleymaniye Camii, with forms radiating from the centre like the petals of a flower, seem to be set in motion by vigorous curves

around the edge. Those in Aya Sofya, 25 feet in diameter and the largest ever made, show the full potential of the "sülüs" style. The calligrapher Kazasker Mustafa Izzet (1801–76) avoided elaborate borders and placed the letters in a dynamic relationship with their plain backgrounds.

Like many of the great calligraphers, Kazasker was a multifaceted individual. A master musician, he was as expert on the reed flute as with the reed pen. The beauty of his voice as a boy had attracted the attention of Mahmut II, who ordered him to be educated in the palace. He learned calligraphy from the great master Yeserizade Kazasker Mustafa Izzet, whose name he later adopted. But he found life in palace service irksome. Absconding by not returning from a pilgrimage to Mecca, he decided to spend his life in prayer and devotion. The sultan, however, recognised Kazasker's voice singing in Beyazit II Camii, forgave him, and brought him back. After holding various positions, such as *imam* at Eyüp, he was appointed by Sultan Abdülmecid as Supreme Judge for Rumelia (European Turkey) and Chief of the *Ulema* (scholars of Islamic Law). He continued to practice calligraphy daily, and taught the royal princes.

The art continued to flourish in the early twentieth century, but in 1928 Atatürk virtually outlawed the Arabic script, and calligraphy in schools ceased. Today, however, some fine calligraphers are at work, and new styles have come from the pens of contemporary masters.

Generally mosque designs based on the aisled hall prevailed, but occasion-
ally domes appeared as a way to emphasise the entrance or the area around
the *mihrab*. Eventually the dome was to emerge as an essential feature in
Ottoman architecture.

Seljuk Architecture

The first Turkic people to develop a strong Islamic tradition in architecture
were the Seljuks who, from their base in Persia, conquered much of Anatolia
in the eleventh century. Their most decisive defeat of Byzantine forces, at
the Battle of Manzikert in 1071, contributed to the decline of the Byzantine
Empire. Although the Seljuk Empire flourished for a while, it was short lived.
Divided between rival generals, it became fragmented and collapsed with
the conquests of the Mongol ruler Genghis Khan after 1243. Nevertheless,
the Seljuks left a significant architectural legacy, building many mosques
and *medreses* (religious schools). They made great use of the dome, constructed spectacular minarets, and were influenced more by the art of
Persia, Turkmenistan and Afghanistan than by the Classical world. As a
result their ornament was elaborate and inventive. The twelfth-century
Ulucami (Great Mosque), built by the Seljuks in Diyarbakır in eastern
Anatolia, follows the tradition of the many-columned hall. It is based on the
Umayyad mosque at Damascus. The horizontal expanse of the interior is
almost the opposite of the centralised Ottoman mosque of the sixteenth
century. Looking down the nave one is almost unaware of the small dome
over the space between the central entrance and the *mihrab*.

The Muqarnas (stalactite vault)

This unique architectural element was invented by Islamic architects. A type
of vault with a structure somewhat like a honeycomb, it gradually projects
from a wall in small steps. Sometimes the effect is of a series of miniature
niches moving progressively forwards and upwards. In other examples it
looks more like stalactites in a cave. In early Ottoman mosques, *muqarnas*
appear on pendentives and they are found almost universally above the portals of mosques and over *mihrabs*. The same form is also adapted to the capitals of columns. This unique means of making a transition, either in stone
or using ceramic tiles, brings surfaces to life as they catch the light.

Mosque windows

In Christian churches windows are generally high in the walls, eliminating
any connection with the outside, but mosques usually have windows near
the floor, so that light enters close to worshippers and creates a view into
the peaceful cemetery garden. Perhaps this feature offers a reminder of
human mortality, but it also creates a human scale and an almost domestic
character. People reading the Qur'an usually choose to be beside these windows where they feel comfortable and can see well. The Ottoman scholar
Evliya Çelebi, describing the Süleymaniye Mosque, wrote that the scent of
flowers filled the prayer hall from open windows, 'perfuming the minds of
the congregation as if they had entered paradise'.

Sokollu Mehmet Paşa
Camii, Kadırga:
This *muqarnas* vault is
over the entrance. The
calligraphic inscription,
the polychrome stone-
work, and the inter-
locking voussoirs of the
arch are all typical of
Ottoman architecture.

THE OTTOMAN EMPIRE

The dynasty of sultans founded by Osman I (*c.*1290–1326) ruled over an empire that, at its peak in the sixteenth century, stretched eastwards from the Balkans through the Middle East to the shores of the Caspian Sea, south to the Persian Gulf, and west along the coast of North Africa to include Egypt and Algeria. The Osmanlı, or Ottomans, began in the thirteenth century as just one of the tribes filling the vacuum after the decline of the Seljuks and the Mongols. Osman I, who claimed independence from the Seljuks in about 1290, continued their practice of spreading Islam while conquering Byzantine territory. The birth and early progress of the empire that he founded is revealed partly through the mosques built by its leaders in their three capitals: Bursa, Edirne and Istanbul. After Selim I conquered Egypt, Syria and Arabia, he assumed the caliphate and thus became the guardian of the holy cities of Mecca and Medina. The role of caliph greatly enhanced the prestige of the sultans who succeeded him. The empire gradually declined during the eighteenth and nineteenth centuries, and came to an end when the last sultan, Mehmet VI Vahideddin, was sent into exile in 1922.

Yeşil Türbe (Green Tomb; see page 32). The tomb of Mehmet I, which stands next to the Yeşil Cami, retains brilliant green tilework that also covered the dome of the mosque.

MOSQUES IN BURSA AND EDİRNE BEFORE THE CONQUEST OF CONSTANTINOPLE

The cities of Bursa and Edirne played pivotal roles in the creation of the Ottoman Empire, and are ideal places to explore early Ottoman architecture. The army of the dying Osman, founder of the Ottoman dynasty, conquered Bursa in April 1326 after a ten-year siege. Osman's son, Orhan Gazi, quickly transformed the city into his capital, and in this way opened an important phase of Ottoman architecture. Bursa's position on the Silk Road and the resulting lucrative silk industry ensured the riches necessary for ambitious building projects.

Thirty-five years later, in 1361, Orhan's son Murat I captured Adrianople, northwest of Constantinople in Thrace. Its name was adapted to Edirne. After the sack of Bursa by the Mongol invader Timur in 1402, Murat moved the capital to Edirne. Meanwhile, Bursa continued to thrive. The proximity of the two cities to Constantinople encouraged the Ottoman rulers to turn them into showcases for their growing empire. Sultans and other high officials considered it their duty to build mosques, and often made them part of the larger complexes known as *külliyes*. These commonly included religious schools, public baths, hospitals, accommodation for travellers and kitchens to feed the poor. Most sultans built tombs for themselves and for their families adjacent to their mosques. As will be seen in some of the examples that are included in this section, *külliyes* were often built on the edges of cities to form the cores of new neighbourhoods.

Ulucami, Bursa. The cluster of small domes is typical of early Ottoman mosques.

ALÂEDDİN CAMİİ (Itinerary H)

Bursa 1335

Alâeddin Camii in Bursa is worth a visit because it conveys the character of the earliest Ottoman mosques. Alâeddin was Orhan Gazi's younger brother, and he built the mosque ten years after the conquest of the city. A small structure, only 8.2 metres square, it is enclosed by plain stone walls supporting a hemi-spherical dome. The shafts and the balcony supports of the minaret may be the oldest in existence. The porch roof stands on four Byzantine columns re-used from a Christian building, a practice rarely followed after this time. Inside, one is very conscious of the simple geometry of the square ground plan and the windowless dome. The only openings are seven small windows in the walls. But one element, however, adds complexity.

The transition from the square to the circle, which was in later buildings achieved by pendentives, is made ingeniously here by a band of triangular planes. This feature, described in more detail below, is known as the "Turkish band of triangles", and was common in early Ottoman mosques.

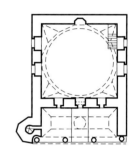

right
Alâeddin Camii: plan
Aptullah Kuran

Pendentives

These are concave, triangular structures that link square walls to the circular base of a dome, commonly used in Byzantine architecture. The sketch below shows the pendentives at Ulucami in Bursa. In early Ottoman architecture, pendentives were sometimes faced with a *muqarnas* design.

Squinches

Spanning the corners of a square space, squinches are arches that turn the square into an octagon. From here the transition to a circle is easy. At Orhan Gazi Camii (opposite), the squinches are filled with unique three-dimensional forms based on triangles.

Turkish band of triangles

In several mosques in Bursa, the transition from square to circle is made using a series of irregular pyramidal forms that appear almost like origami. This ingenious architectural device takes various forms. The sketch below shows Yeşil Cami in Bursa (see page 30).

Orhan built this mosque thirteen years after the conquest, choosing a site on open land outside the walled citadel. The mosque was part of a complex which included a *medrese*, a bath and a soup kitchen, as well as a commercial building to raise revenues in support of the charitable elements of the complex. Only the mosque and the bath survive, but the sultan's city planning strategy clearly worked. The market district around it flourishes today as the centre of the modern city.

Orhan Gazi Camii is of a mosque type derived from Seljuk *medreses*. Three or four large spaces, known as *eyvans*, open off a central court through broad arches. Here, in this Ottoman adaptation, the court is not open to the sky but is covered by a dome. On three sides of this space, which functions as a central hall, arches lead to domed *eyvans* with raised floors. The principal *eyvan* opposite the entrance, which contains the *mihrab*, is the main prayer hall, while those on either side were intended for personal prayer.

A remarkable feature of Orhan Gazi Camii is the variety of different ways in which it makes the transition from the rectangular lines of the ground plan to the domes. In the central hall, pendentives transform the square plan into an octagon, above which round, arched windows alternate with fan-shaped panels of triangles pointing upwards towards the dome. In the prayer hall, a band of eight pointed arches form an octagon beneath the dome. Four of them act as squinches, cutting across the corners of the square, and these are filled with an amazing pattern of triangular planes (resembling elaborate origami designs). As a change from such elaboration, the domes of the side *eyvans* are carried on pendentives alone.

Such experimentation indicates that the architect was likely to have been fascinated by the decorative potential of structural devices. The mosque was restored after a fire in the fifteenth century and an earthquake in 1855, but it remains close to its original form.

Orhan Gazi Camii:
Exterior. The domes on
octagonal drums over
square walls reveal the
interior form.

Beyazit I was known as "Yıldırım", meaning "thunderbolt", because of the astonishing speed with which he moved across his territories. He built this mosque and its *külliye* on a hill to the east of the city. One can see that the city grew around it, as was intended. The mosque is of the same three-*eyvan* type as Orhan Gazi Camii. Here the central hall and the three *eyvans* are again domed, and transitions from square to circle are made in a variety of ways. The prayer hall contains an excellent example of the Turkish band of triangles. Convent rooms, in the corners of the mosque, are entered through small doors from the central hall. These rooms were built to house travelling dervishes.

The *medrese* that accompanied it is now a medical clinic.

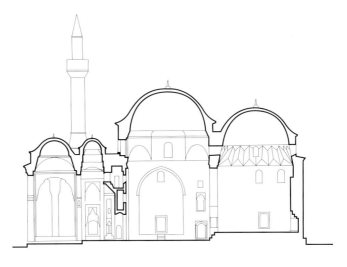

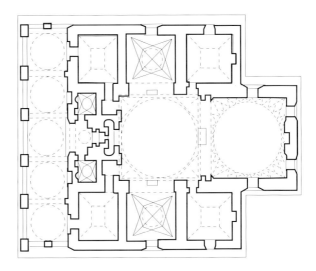

4 ULUCAMİ (Itinerary H)
(Great Mosque)

Bursa 1396–1400

With his customary "thunderbolt" speed, Beyazit I began the nearby Ulucami the next year after Yıldırım Beyazit Camii was completed. It was built to celebrate the sultan's decisive victory over the forces of a European crusader army at Nicopolis on the Danube. Financed by the valuable booty won there, the mosque was intended for Friday prayers for the whole population of Bursa. Since extremely large domes had not yet been attempted, his architect simply increased the number of small ones. Legend has it that Beyazit had promised he would build 20 mosques if he won the battle of Nicopolis, but he was persuaded by a wise dervish that a mosque with 20 domes would suffice.

The high limestone walls of the exterior, which border the market, are relatively plain. Two minarets on the north side, facing the market, proclaim the function of the build-ing, and a *muqarnas* portal on the same side gives entrance to the central aisle. The astonishing interior is revealed gradually as one moves through it. Twelve great piers, along with buttresses on the surrounding walls, support 20 domes of equal diameter. Carried simply on pendentives, each one is penetrated by eight small windows. The effect is of an immense horizontal space, whose repeated piers impart a sense of gravity and order. Between them, five aisles running east–west and four running north–south seem to disappear into the distance. Pools of light under the domes enliven the long vistas. On the central axis from the entrance to the *mihrab* the domes are raised on slightly higher drums; the second one in from the portal is the highest of all. Beneath it is an unusual *şadırvan*. This elegant marble fountain, with water cascading from bowl to bowl, dates from the nineteenth century. The original open oculus in the centre of the dome was enclosed in glass in the same century. However, the activity of the faithful washing before prayer in this place goes back 500 years.

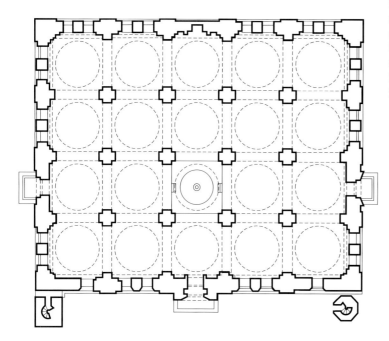

opposite
Ulucami: night view. The dark forms of many domes can be seen above the floodlit walls. See also the view on page 21.

left
Ulucami: plan. The entrance from the market, between the minarets, leads to the fountain in the second bay and to the *mihrab* at the end of the central aisle. *Aptullah Kuran*

Another strong visual accent is given by the calligraphy on the piers, whose vigorous but delicate forms contrast with the solidity of the structure.

The plan of the Ulucami, with its many piers breaking up the space, appears to revert to the horizontal layout of the great mosques of North Africa and the Middle East and of the Seljuk mosques of Anatolia. But we need not think of it as a design purely rooted in the past. Beyazit and his unknown architect created a new spirit of monumentality and spatial order. It deserves to be experienced

on its own terms as one of the great interior spaces of Ottoman architecture. While, for example, the Seljuk Ulucami at Diyarbakır is relatively dark, the space here is flooded with light. While at Diyarbakır the aisles run only in one direction, the many intersecting aisles at Bursa create a continuity of space throughout the mosque. At the same time, each domed bay seems to stand on its own. This infusion of daylight into interior space, along with the opening up of that space, was to become a guiding principle of mosque design in the future.

There is a popular story about the şadırvan of the Ulucami. When Yıldırım Beyazit decided to build the mosque, a lady who was either Jewish or Christian lived in one of the houses on the land. She did not consent to sell her house to the Sultan for the building of the mosque. But she soon died and when the mosque was built a fountain rather than a worshipping area was placed where her house used to stand.

The Bursa Ulucami represents an early peak in Ottoman power. Within two years of its completion Beyazit I had lost the Battle of Ankara against

the dreaded Timur (Tamerlane), the Mongol conqueror. Beyazit I died in captivity in 1403. For the next eleven years Beyazit's three sons fought with each other over the succession. The breakup of Timur's empire after his death in 1405 made way for the future expansion of the Ottoman Empire.

above left
Ulucami: Interior. The massive piers support 20 equal domes.

above
Ulucami: The elegant marble *şadırvan* from the nineteenth century.

5 YEŞİL CAMİ (Itinerary H)
(Green Mosque)
Bursa 1412–22

Yeşil Cami, Bursa: plan and section. From left to right, porch (not built), vestibule with stairs to the sultan's lodge, central hall with fountain and arches opening to lateral *eyvans*, prayer hall. *Aptullah Kuran*

Yeşil Cami is significant as the first Ottoman mosque to be decorated with ceramic tiles. It was begun by Beyazit's son Mehmet I, before he defeated his brothers and assumed the sultanate in 1413. Its architectural brilliance seems to confirm his rise to power.

The innovation of interior surfaces brought to life with richly coloured tiles may have resulted from Timur's invasion of Bursa. Nakkaş Ali (Ali the designer), who was responsible for much of the tilework, appears to have been to Samarkand, where Timur's palace and many other buildings were lined with fine tiles. While it is said that the tileworkers came from Tabriz in Persia, the techniques they used suggest Samarkand as a more likely source.

Yeşil Cami is of the same *eyvan* type as Orhan Gazi Camii (page 23) and Yıldırım Beyazit Camii (page 24), and all its main spaces are domed. It also contains four convent rooms in the corners. Although the porch was never built, the entrance is through a beautiful *muqarnas* portal in the marble façade. You will pass through a vestibule with tiled walls into a small barrel-vaulted *eyvan*, and then into the covered court with a pool under a lantern in the dome. From here the space opens through arches, up four steps into the prayer hall, and on the same level into the other *eyvans*. It is clear that the central hall was not intended as part of the sacred space of the mosque, because there are niches in the steps leading up to the main *eyvan*, in which the faithful could leave their shoes. The two domes on the main axis are supported on fine Turkish bands of triangles, while those of the side *eyvans* are on squinches decorated with stalactites.

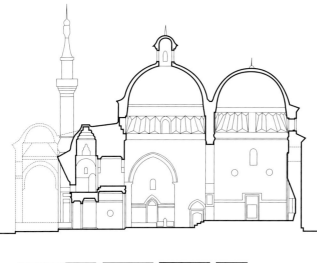

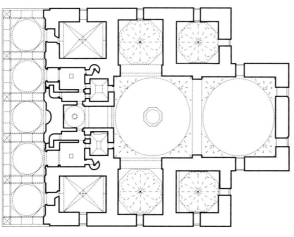

opposite
Yeşil Cami, Bursa: View from the prayer hall to the central hall. The richly tiled sultan's lodge is above the arched entrance. One *eyvan* opens to the right. Note the Turkish band making the transition from the square walls to the dome.

The interior is enriched with deep green tiles that were once gilded. The tilework reaches its peak in the beautiful *mihrab*, where the green is accented by blue, white and yellow. Surrounded by an elaborate geometric border, sinuous plant forms adorn the flat surfaces of the front, and six tiers of stalactites cover the niche. This "gate of paradise" is an auspicious beginning to a great tradition in ceramic decoration.

Turn back towards the entrance to see a large recess in the upper wall, like a fourth *eyvan*, raised up to overlook the whole interior. This is the sultan's lodge, fronted by an elegant, ceramic balustrade with star-shaped openings, richly tiled, and decorated with a painted and gilded ceiling. The sultan's family would worship behind the latticed windows on either side of the lodge, the men on the east side and the women to the west. The larger recesses in the wall below were for courtiers. This was the first mosque to include special places for the sultan and his family. Exiting the vestibule one will notice superb tiling and see the anterooms on either side from which the staircases go up to the royal quarters. It is easy to imagine the sumptuously attired sultan and his retinue arriving, with a throng of people waiting to petition him.

The exteriors of the domes were originally embellished with green tiles; now they are covered in lead. Some vestiges of the former splendour remains in the marble window surrounds of inlaid turquoise tiles. Mehmet's splendid tomb, however, next to the mosque, retains most of the green tiles that gave it the name of Yeşil Türbe (Green Tomb).

opposite
Yeşil Türbe (Green Tomb), Bursa: Built for Mehmet I, it retains much of its original tile work. (See also page 20.)

above

Muradiye Camii, Bursa: Prayer hall with *mihrab* and *minber*. The complex *muqarnas* design that begins the transition to the dome can be seen faintly in the corner.

above right

Muradiye Camii from the south across a cemetery

Murat II, who reigned, except for a two-year interruption, for 30 years (1421–51), was a great warrior. Although he was unsuccessful in his siege of Constantinople, he wrested Salonika from the Venetians and invaded Greece. His greatest military success was at Varna, where in 1422 he defeated crusaders led by Ladislaus III of Poland and Hungary. After this victory he withdrew from the life of a soldier to spend his time with Ottoman scholars, theologians and poets. Interested in the development of the Turkish language (neg-

lected in intellectual circles in favour of Persian and Arabic), Murat II also encouraged the study of Turkish history, particularly romantic stories about the exploits of his ancestors.

This mosque was built early in his reign. It is entered through a porch with tiled decoration in the spandrels above the arches. It follows the typical Bursa plan with three *eyvans* arranged similarly to those at Orhan Gazi Camii. However, the support of the two main domes, each different from the other, is made in a most elaborate way. Architects in Bursa

had already experimented with a wide range of techniques, but the designer of this mosque appears to have attempted to eclipse all his predecessors.

In the first *eyvan* the transition from square to circular is made by a complex construction of triangles that seems to continue the geometry of the Turkish band down into the corners. A completely novel system is used in the second *eyvan*, in which convex pendentives, surfaced with a *muqarnas* design, bulge out from the corners below a Turkish band.

Muradiye Camii can be seen as the last fling of those who exploited this kind of complexity to create the aura of a sultan's mosque. The essence of the architecture that was to follow depended not so much on surface elaboration as the expansion of space through structural ingenuity. Murat II's next major mosque, Üç Şerefeli Cami in Edirne, takes a major step towards that new goal.

Muradiye Camii, Bursa: view from the southwest, showing the two equal domes of the central hall and prayer hall. To the right is the lower dome of an *eyvan*.

ESKİ CAMİ (Itinerary J)

(Old Mosque)
Edirne Begun 1403

Eski Cami, Edirne:
The polychrome arches
of the interior create an
architectural character
that differs from the
Ulucami in Bursa.
The calligraphy makes
a powerful impact.

The Eski Cami in Edirne was begun by Beyazit I's son Süleyman, while he was asserting his claim to the sultanate in Edirne after the breakup of the Ottoman domains following Timur's defeat of Beyazit. Süleyman must have been familiar with the 20-domed Ulucami in Bursa and presumably asked his architect Hacı Alaettin to build one like it. However, lacking his father's resources, he limited the number of domes to nine. The domes are arranged within a perfect square. Unlike the mosque in Bursa, this one is entered through a porch. At Bursa the second bay inside the portal was an open court with a fountain, whereas in Edirne the fountain was probably in the first bay to allow space for prayer in front of the *mihrab*. Today the fountain is gone and the floor carpeted. The slightly smaller piers and wider span of the arches than those in Bursa give the interior a very different character, as does the strong polychrome painting on the arches that simulates alternate blocks of red and white stone. While all the domes rest on plain pendentives in Bursa, there is a striking variety here. The first dome of the centre row is on squinches; the second on stalactites, and the third, closest to the *mihrab*, on a Turkish band. The others are on pendentives. Süleyman did not survive to see his mosque finished; it was completed by his brother, Mehmet I. Within a few decades it was supplanted as the Friday mosque by the Üç Şerefeli Cami and for that reason became the Eski Cami (Old Mosque).

8 MURADİYE CAMİİ (Itinerary J)

Edirne 1435

Murat II originally built this structure as a convent for dervishes of the Mevlevî order (known as the Whirling Dervishes), but it was converted into a mosque later in his reign. It is the best representative in Edirne of a Bursa type, the *eyvan* mosque, consisting of a central hall and three *eyvans*. The three extensions, each with a dome, can be seen from the outside, clustered around the square central block with its larger dome. The spatial clarity of the interior is impressive. Originally the central hall contained a fountain and its floor was at a lower level. Its dome is supported on a Turkish band of triangles. One of the chief reasons to visit this mosque is to see the early fifteenth-century tiles that were probably made by the same craftsmen who worked in the Yeşil Cami in Bursa. The spectacular *mihrab* of "cuerda seca" tiles (see page 89) is covered with a blue and white tiled *muqarnas* vault using the underglaze method. This appears to be the first experimental use of this technique that was to be employed in the İznik potteries at the peak of their success. On the north wall is a panel of hexagonal blue and white tiles with turquoise triangles between them. Both the *muqarnas* vault and the wall panel show a Chinese influence, which is not surprising at a time when Chinese porcelain was reaching Turkey by the Silk Road. However, these tiles are not mere imitations, but early and excellent examples of an intrinsically Ottoman style.

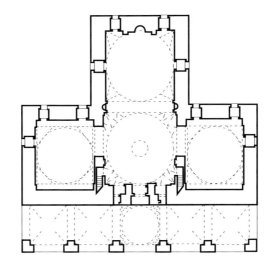

Muradiye Camii, Edirne: A typical three-*eyvan* plan.

9   ÜÇ ŞEREFELİ CAMİ (Itinerary J)
(Three-Balconied Mosque)
Edirne 1438–47

On the west side of this mosque, the plain limestone façade gradually steps up from the courtyard on the left to the mosque on the right. The domed arcade of the court nearest the mosque is slightly higher than the rest. To the right are two smaller domes, with the central one rising behind. The most striking elements of the exterior are the two minarets on this side. The highest one, to the south with three balconies and giving the mosque its name, is decorated with a diamond pattern from the base to the first balcony. This was the tallest minaret in the Ottoman realm until Selimiye Camii was built, close by, 130 years later. The minaret in the northwest corner spirals up dramatically to the only balcony, while the other two are enriched with different designs.

As already seen, early Ottoman architects experimented with a variety of plans, structural systems and decorative schemes. Their inventiveness reached a new peak, however, in Üç Şerefeli Cami, built under the patronage of Murat II. Major innovations made it a pivotal design, and paved the way to the mosques of the sixteenth century. One of these is the separation of the court from the mosque. In the *eyvan*-type mosques in Bursa, the domed courts opening through arches to three or more *eyvans* were secular spaces, containing fountains, within the body of the mosque. This can best be seen in the Yeşil Cami, where the fountain survives. In the Bursa Ulucami the fountain court, in the second bay on the axis from the main portal to the *mihrab*, was also integrated within the building. However, at Üç Şerefeli Cami the court is open to the sky as an autonomous space, making the transition from the busy streets of the city into the sacred interior of the prayer hall. It is surrounded on all four sides by shady arcades, much like a medieval cloister. At its centre is the fountain. While the open court was not new to Islamic architecture (it was common in the mosques of North Africa and the Middle East, and appeared at the Ulucami in Manisa in 1376), the court at Üç Şerefeli Cami, built in the Ottoman capital shortly before the conquest of Constantinople, was to be extremely influential.

A second innovation is the size and dominance of the dome. For the first time, the centre of the prayer hall was covered by a really large dome, while pairs of smaller domes shelter subsidiary spaces on either side. The main dome span is 24.10 metres, almost twice the size of those of Yeşil Cami. The plan shows the clear hierarchy between the major prayer hall beneath it and the minor areas that extend the space to either side. A curious feature is that miniscule domes have been inserted into the four triangles between large and small domes.

above
Üç Şerefeli Cami, Edirne:
The first large Ottoman
dome. It is carried on
eight supports, and the
transition from octagon
to circle is made in a
unique manner with a
muqarnas design.

right
Üç Şerefeli Cami:
Plan and section. The
courtyard with fountain
is an exterior space,
surrounded by arcaded
walks. For the first time
a large dome dominates
the centre of the prayer
hall, while smaller
domes cover subsidiary
spaces to the sides.
Aptullah Kuran

CONVERTED CHRISTIAN CHURCHES

Byzantine churches possessed a unique character. By the early sixth century their architects had turned away from the long basilicas of Early Christian Italy to create centrally planned, domed structures. Their delicately carved capitals, marble revetments and representational mosaics gave the interiors a magical quality. The rich ornamentation of their surfaces seemed to dissolve solid walls into images of heaven. In response to the Christian liturgy, churches tended to be divided into a series of separate spatial compartments. The prohibition, in the Islamic religion, of any images of humans or animals, as well as the need to orient the *mihrab* towards Mecca, meant that churches had to be transformed before they met the needs of Muslim worship. In this chapter we will see how three churches were adapted into mosques, and later chapters will show the profound influence of Hagia Sophia on Ottoman mosques.

10 AYA SOFYA (Itinerary A)

1453
(Hagia Sophia, 532–37)

above
Aya Sofya surrounded by its four minarets. This view from one of the minarets of the Sultan Ahmet Camii shows its superb position crowning the First Hill.

opposite
The Sultan's lodge to the left, the calligraphic roundel, above right, and the *müezzin mahfili*, a platform from which the *müezzin* chants during prayers, all show the conversion of the church into a mosque.

One of Mehmet the Conqueror's first acts, after entering Constantinople on May 29 1453, was to convert the Byzantine church of Hagia Sophia into a mosque. His great grandfather, Beyazit I, longed to fulfil the Prophet Muhammad's prophecy that one day Muslims would conquer Constantinople. Beyazit had set his hopes on taking possession of Hagia Sophia for Islam, and besieged the city from 1394 until he was forced to defend his realm against Timur. But Beyazit only beheld this masterpiece of Byzantine architecture from a distance. Almost 60 years were to pass before Mehmet II entered the walls and rode to Hagia Sophia to claim the symbolic prize. The court historian, Tursun Beg, describes Mehmet's visit to the church and his astonishment at the splendour of the dome that "competes with the dome of the Heavens". Admiring the coloured marble floor and the dome covered with "tiny, colourful pieces of glass and golden rock crystals", Tursun continued: "When one looks from its floor to its ceiling, he sees the sky filled with stars, and when one looks from the ceiling to the floor he sees the seas with dashing waves." After Mehmet had "observed the interesting and strange arts and images" inside Hagia Sophia, "the sultan of the universe" climbed to the dome. The words of the Prophet must have echoed through his head as he gazed over the city from the top of this architectural wonder: "They will conquer Constantinople. Hail to the prince and the army to whom this is granted." Many earlier Byzantine churches had been built in the eastern Roman Empire, and the Ottomans were familiar with some of them, but this church eclipsed all its predecessors. Mehmet immediately commanded that it be repaired and made into a royal mosque. The next Friday the *müezzin* gave the call to prayer from a temporary wooden minaret, probably an adaptation of a bell tower. With the sultan in attendance, Aya Sofya was initiated as a place of Islamic worship. During the next two centuries, it exerted a profound influence on Ottoman architecture.

Justinian's church

Hagia Sophia (the Church of Holy Wisdom) expressed the ambitions of the Emperor Justinian (483–565), who had revived the splendour of the Byzantine Empire after many years of decline. The church was the crowning achievement of a "golden age" of both military conquest and magnificent architecture. Its two architects were mathematicians. Anthemios of Thralles was an expert in geometry and an inventor, and Isidorus of Miletus was a professor of physics at the universities of Alexandria and Constantinople. Neither was a master builder, but they possessed the vision necessary to conceive such a grand project. They relied on the knowledge of skilled builders, and doubtless gave them alarming challenges as they pushed the boundaries of structural design.

Hagia Sophia was a new departure in architecture. With amazing daring, the architects combined the characteristics of two Roman types: the centralised domed rotunda and the basilica with its long central nave. More specifically, it seems as if they combined the structural

principles of two major Roman buildings, the Pantheon and the Basilica of Constantine. The Pantheon, with a dome of solid concrete that was 20 feet thick at the base, relied on sheer mass to remain standing. Its builders did not dare to penetrate the dome with windows, but left a huge oculus in the centre. The entry of light solely through the oculus tends to emphasise the centralisation. The Basilica of Constantine, with a long nave of three vaulted bays, was also of heavy concrete, but it was a more dynamic structure. While in the Pantheon the weight of the dome is transferred equally to the walls all around, the roof of the

Basilica was supported on vast piers in the corners of the vaulting bays. As a result, huge windows could be opened in the high arches that carry the vaults. Thus the interior was flooded with light. The 32-metre (112 feet) span of the dome of Hagia Sophia is less than that of the Pantheon, but it is the centrepiece of a more spacious whole.

At Hagia Sophia, Anthemios and Isidorus planned a central, domed space, but they elongated it with half domes on the east and west sides, thus creating a long nave. They further extended the long axis to the east by the addition of an apse (a semi-circular sanctuary behind

opposite
The thirteenth-century Deisis mosaic in the gallery was exposed for all to see when Aya Sofya became a museum.

right
Plan at gallery level.

below
Gaspare Fossati's nineteenth-century view from the north aisle looking south across the central space.

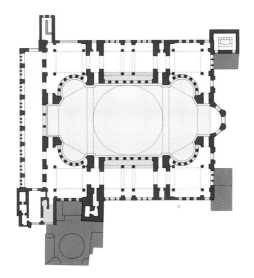

overleaf
The vast calligraphic roundels flanking the southeast exedra proclaim Aya Sofya's conversion to a mosque.

the altar). The result is a unique combination of centralised and longitudinal space. The dome is supported on four massive piers and the transition from the square, with the piers in its corners, to the circular base of the dome is made by pendentives. The complexity of the plan is increased by the addition of curved bays, flanking the spaces under the half domes. These areas, known as "exedrae", are defined by two tiers of curved arcades. Further arcades between the main structural piers separate the central nave from the aisles and galleries on either side. Huge, exterior buttresses on the north and south sides, and the half domes to the east and west, help to resist the colossal outward thrust of the dome.

The ambitious nature of the spatial and structural concept was matched by the quality of the detail, particularly the exquisite carving of the capitals. The delicate foliage, looking like young plant life in the spring, is characteristic of Byzantine architecture. Since Islamic craftsmen had developed their own styles of capitals long before the conquest, such forms will not be seen in the mosques of Istanbul. However, the Ottoman architects did follow the practice of using rich marble and porphyry for columns. Like their Byzantine predecessors, they could draw from quarries of a vast empire, and sometimes they also re-used columns from ancient buildings.

The church was built in the amazingly short period of five years. Two teams of 5000 workers, each supervised by 50 masters, competed as they built opposite sides. Changes were made by the architects as construction proceeded, and they used all their ingenuity to lighten the structure. The dome was built of 40 ribs of solid masonry, between which was an infill of lightweight bricks. As a great advance over the Pantheon, the architects inserted a ring of windows between the ribs at the base of the dome, and penetrated the tympanum walls with countless windows. The gold mosaics on the dome and the vaults, and the marble that covered the walls, reflected the light from many sources and created an astonishing appearance of luminosity. So dazzling was the effect that the Roman historian Procopius wrote of the gleaming reflections: "Indeed one might say that its interior is lit not by the sun from without, but by a radiance generated within." Justinian, gazing upon the church he had commissioned, is credited with saying, "Solomon, I have outdone you."

Hagia Sophia was the result of an experimental design, for which there was no precedent. For all their theoretical knowledge, the architects had no means of calculating the stresses in the dome or in the supporting arches and piers. In fact, they made the dome dangerously shallow. The buttresses on two sides, which had been added after construction began, proved unequal to their task, and they were not perfectly balanced by the half domes on the other sides. Only 30 years after completion, in 557, the structure was weakened by an earthquake. The dome collapsed a year later. Within five years, it was rebuilt 20 feet higher, and closer in form to

a hemisphere. In 869 the western half dome was damaged again, and further earthquakes in 1343 and 1344 caused the collapse in 1346 of parts of the dome and the eastern half dome. Considering its great age and the punishment it has received from several earthquakes, the design of Hagia Sophia can hardly be called a failure. It stands as a testament to the ingenuity of the original designers. But Ottoman architects must have analysed it with a view to creating more efficient structures. How they rose to that challenge can be seen in later chapters of this book.

Conversion to a Mosque
When Mehmet converted Hagia Sophia to a mosque, its name became Aya Sofya. The orientation towards Mecca was asserted by placing the *mihrab* slightly to the right in the apse and turning it ten degrees from the original axis. The *minber* was oriented in the same direction. In addition, two broad steps at the opening to the apse are angled so that they lie parallel to the *mihrab*. As potent symbols of the triumph of Islam, prayer carpets once owned by the Prophet Muhammad and banners of victory were hung on the walls on both sides of the *mihrab*.

Of course, the Christian imagery in mosaics throughout the building presented a problem. With typical Byzantine majesty, a mosaic head of Christ as Pantocrator looked down from the centre of the dome. Mehmet I's historian Tursun, avoiding its true significance as an image of Christ, described it as the head of "a venerable man". But its power was not lost on Mehmet, who remarked that the eyes followed wherever one went. Islamic law proscribed such images, but it was

not immediately removed. It was covered in 1609 by Ahmet I, who interpreted Islamic principles in a rigorous way. Christian mosaics at the lower level were covered over, but others remained in the galleries until the seventeenth century. The mosaic of the Virgin Mary and Jesus in the conch above the apse was never covered. According to one legendary account, it was allowed to remain because the Prophet revered Mary, and spared a representation of the Virgin and Child when he destroyed all the other images in the Ka'ba at Mecca. The rather mysterious forms of four seraphim in the pendentives have also survived. In the course of the various restorations that occurred since the conquest, the decorations on vaults were redone in sympathy with the geometric, non-figural manner of Justinian's time.

Dramatic changes were made to the use of the interior. As the principal patriarchal seat of Eastern Christendom the original church had been a place of elaborate ritual in which a multitude of clergy and high officials took part. After a procession of the bishop and clergy, the emperor, accompanied by members of his court, would make his entrance through the royal portal in the narthex and process along the nave to his throne in the south aisle. During mass, the clergy remained invisible in the chancel behind the curtains of the iconostasis, a screen enclosing the apse and a rectangle before it. At times some of them emerged to read the scriptures from the ambo or pulpit that stood before the entrance to the chancel. At a focal point in the service the emperor would enter the inner sanctuary with the patriarch to bless the bread and wine upon the altar. His unique right to take this role rested on his perceived status as an equal to Christ's apostles. Both he and the patriarch reflected the holiness and the power of God. The central space under the dome was like a stage through which processions passed as a sumptuous spectacle, while the laity looked on from aisles and galleries. Women occupied the galleries while the men were packed into the aisles. Since the structural piers are massive and the arcades between them present something of a barrier, there is a sense of separation between the nave and the surrounding spaces. In Muslim worship, the sultan, even in his role as caliph, did not claim God-like qualities. Without a liturgy, performed ritually by many priests and acolytes, Ottoman needs were different. The altar, pulpit and other church furnishings were cleared away to leave unencumbered space for prayer. Mehmet II built a minaret (no longer existing) on a turret in the southwest corner to the right of the entrance, and another, of brick, in the southeast corner.

Throughout the centuries, sultans continued to revere and maintain Aya Sofya. Beyazit II (1481–1512) added a minaret in the northeast corner. Süleyman the Magnificent (1520–66) flanked the *mihrab* with two giant candlesticks, taken as war trophies from the cathedral at Buda during his Hungarian campaign. His son, Selim II (1566–74), commanded the great sixteenth-century architect Mimar Sinan to make substantial improvements to the structure. He cleared away houses clustered around it, strengthened buttresses, and, finding that Mehmet II's first minaret put too much strain on the structure below, began to replace

it with a new one further from the dome. Sinan also built a magnificent tomb for Selim II beside Aya Sofya. The sultan's desire to be buried there was a further sign of reverence for the former church. His successor Murat III (1574–95) completed the minaret begun by Selim and was persuaded by Sinan to complete the symmetry by adding a fourth of identical design. In addition to their main function the new minarets helped to buttress the corners. Murat III also built a *müezzin mahfili*, a raised platform, near the southeast pier, from which the *müezzin* could chant during prayers. His tomb stands beside that of Selim. Mahmut I (1730–54) carried out restoration work and added a beautiful library in the south aisle. Its reading room, lined with İznik tiles, can be seen through a bronze grille. Mahmut was also responsible for the elegant fountain that stands to the south of the main entrance, and added a school for children nearby.

The last major Ottoman restoration (1847–49) was carried out by the Swiss architects Gaspare and Giuseppe Fossati, in the reign of Sultan Abdülmecid. At this time mosaics previously covered in the galleries were revealed, admired by the sultan, and carefully covered so as not to destroy them. The Fossatis' work, in addition to major repairs, included the building of the sultan's lodge against the northeast pier. They are well-known today for the fine coloured renderings they made of the restored building.

The calligraphy, installed by the Fossati brothers, gives the building its strongest sign of identity as a mosque. The huge roundels that hang high up on the four piers are the work of Kazasker Mustafa Izzet. As in many mosques, the roundels bear the sacred names of God, the Prophet

Muhammad, Abu Bakr, Umar, Osman, Ali, Hasan and Husein. The inscription running round the crown of the dome, by the same calligrapher, reads: "In the name of God the Merciful and Compassionate; God is the light of Heaven and Earth. The light is Himself and not that which shines through glass or gleams in the morning star or glows in the firebrand."

In later chapters we shall see how, after the conquest, Ottoman architects opened up space in their mosques by reducing the mass of the structural piers and minimising the separation of nave and aisles. Thus they created more egalitarian prayer halls. Their admiration of Aya Sofya was, nevertheless, profound. The awe in which the Ottomans held it is demonstrated in an extraordinary legend. It is said that early in the seventh century, when one of the half domes collapsed, none of Constantinople's master builders knew how to rebuild it. They decided to send ambassadors to seek advice from the Prophet Muhammad. The mission was successful, for not only did they return with a formula for its reconstruction, but also a special mortar that included sand from Mecca and some of the Prophet's saliva. This story, scarcely credible because no collapse occurred during the lifetime of the Prophet, makes it clear that the Ottomans desperately wanted some Islamic legitimacy for their newly acquired masterpiece. The truth is that the sultans, accepting Christ's role as a prophet of Islam, perceived continuity in Aya Sofya's status, both as a place of worship and a symbol of imperial power. Furthermore, the visionary ideal of creating a luminous space under a celestial dome lived on in their own architecture, to reach a peak in the sixteenth century.

11 KÜÇÜK AYASOFYA CAMİİ (Itinerary A)
SS. Sergius and Bacchus c.526

The small church of SS. Sergius and Bacchus, which stands close to the shore of the Sea of Marmara below the Sultan Ahmet Camii, is the second most important of Justinian's age. The date of its construction is uncertain, but it has long been considered a prelude to the design of Hagia Sophia. The same architects may even have been involved. Certainly, the innovative nature of the design suggests the intellectual approach of theorists, rather than the work of traditional master builders. It is perhaps best known as a prototype for the important church of San Vitale in Ravenna (547), which celebrated Justinian's reconquest of northeastern Italy.

SS. Sergius and Bacchus is octagonal, with eight piers supporting a dome somewhat similar in exterior form to that of Hagia Sophia. An ambulatory and galleries surround the central space. The openings between the piers, divided by slender columns, are alternately curved, like those in the exedrae at Hagia Sophia, and straight. The shafts of the columns are of green marble in the curved bays and red marble in the straight ones. The lower tiers carry an architrave, while those above are arched. The effect is of a marvelously fluid space, not confined by a rigid octagon, but flowing into recesses between the piers. The dome is most unusual in its construction. Somewhat like the top of a pumpkin, the upper surface billows out between sixteen ribs, but the segments are alternately flat and curved. Such a scheme was not used again. The complexity of the design

SS. Sergius and Bacchus: The octagonal space converted to a Muslim prayer hall. The *minber* stands in the foreground.

seems quintessentially Byzantine, in a way that differentiates it from most Ottoman architecture. The carved capitals and architraves are of beautiful craftsmanship. A band of Greek inscriptions can still be seen at the base of the dome.

Mehmet II permitted Christians and Jews to follow their own faiths. This church remained as a Christian place of worship until the sixteenth century, when it was converted into a mosque under the direction of Hüseyin Ağa, the chief black eunuch of Beyazit II. The *mihrab* and *minber* were added, with their orientation

towards Mecca. Christian symbols were removed. The gold mosaics and marble revetments disappeared, making it hard to visualise the original appearance. Eighteenth-century decorations over the arches fronting the galleries are inappropriate to the Byzantine design. A porch in the traditional Ottoman style was added.

While Aya Sofya's influence on the mosques of Istanbul is generally recognised, SS. Sergius and Bacchus is often overlooked in this respect. Mimar Sinan built several octagonal mosques, and it is hard to believe that he did not study this church and

consider how to modify the structural scheme to meet his own architectural goals. If you make the short walk up the hill to his beautiful Sokollu Mehmet Paşa Camii, you will see that this followed a hexagonal plan more than a thousand years after SS. Sergius and Bacchus was built.

SS. Sergius and
Bacchus: View from the
southwest.

CHURCH OF THEOTOKOS KYRIOTISSA (Itinerary B)

6th–12th centuries

Kalenderhane Cami *c.*1453

This brick structure was based on the Greek cross, the most typical plan for small Byzantine churches, with its four equal arms around a central domed space. This is not an arrangement favoured for Ottoman mosques, and it is interesting to see how different it is from others in the city. It is also worth visiting because it shows the difficulties of adaptation. The *mihrab* is placed across one corner of the eastern arm of the cross and the *minber* is similarly oriented. The change of direction is awkward, and is emphasised further by bold stripes on the carpet that run obliquely to the Byzantine axis.

The extreme age of this church is made plain by the level of the paving outside, which has risen far above the original floor. Some of the marble revetment remains inside, but any mosaics or frescoes on the dome and vaults have long disappeared. It was converted during the reign of Mehmet II for use as a *tekke* (lodge) for dervishes of the Kalender order, hence its current name.

Kalenderhane Cami. The outward form is typical of small Byzantine churches.

EARLY MOSQUES AFTER THE CONQUEST

Immediately after the conquest, Mehmet II provided places of worship by converting Christian churches into mosques. These sufficed for the initial Muslim population, and priority was given to such vital necessities as fortifications and water supply. Since the palaces of the Byzantine rulers were in ruins, Mehmet was also engaged in building a fitting palace, on the Third Hill, for himself and his court.

Mehmet II pursued a vigorous policy of moving people to his capital, and within a few years the construction of new mosques became necessary. At first, they were modelled on traditional Ottoman types, with some Byzantine principles. However, within half a century the influence of Aya Sofya grew stronger.

Mahmut Paşa was one of Mehmet's grand viziers, and was the first to commission a new mosque in the city. He came from an aristocratic Greek family who had gone over to the Ottoman side after the conquest. On the Black Sea coast he secured the surrender of the last Byzantine Emperor, David Comnemus, and two years later he distinguished himself by capturing King Stephen of Bosnia. At the height of his power, enriched by war booty, he was in a position to build a fine mosque. It was fortunate that he proceeded quickly with the construction of his own tomb, for he succumbed to the sultan's wrath and was executed in 1474 after a disastrous defeat in the Upper Euphrates region of Anatolia.

The original appearance of the porch was lost when its six columns were encased in heavier masonry after a fire in 1827, but the interior

right
Mahmut Paşa Camii: View into the twin domes of the prayer hall. Both domes are supported on pendentives.

opposite
Sultan Beyazit II Camii: The central dome on pendentives, the half dome, lower left, and the tympanum wall on the right, all penetrated by windows, show the influence of Aya Sofya.

still retains its historic form. As you stand within it, you will see that this mosque belongs to an earlier era than most of those in Istanbul. With its two-domed prayer hall, it is an adaptation of the Bursa type found in the Yeşil Cami (see page 30), but it lacks the *eyvans* opening off the central space. From the porch you enter a five-bay narthex (vestibule), which has a central dome resting on *muqarnas*, flanked by scalloped domes. Those in the end bays are supported on Turkish bands of triangles. The domes of the spacious prayer hall, 12.5 metres in diameter, are supported on plain pendentives.

Three domed rooms, which lead off passages on each side, were originally used to accommodate travelling dervishes. Those on the left, devoid of decoration and simply whitewashed, are accessible and worth seeing. The architect was Atik Sinan (Sinan the elder), who should not be confused with the sixteenth-century architect Sinan the Great.

Mahmut Paşa's tomb is unique in the use of a lively and colourful mosaic of tiles on its exterior. Although the tiles are probably from İznik (a centre of pottery production), the pattern in which they are arranged is reminiscent of Moorish design.

Mahmut Paşa Camii: Plan. This is a modified version of the Bursa type without the *eyvans*. *Aptullah Kuran*

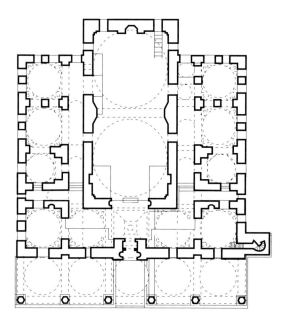

14 FATİH CAMİİ (Itinerary F)

Mehmet the Conqueror's mosque and complex 1463–70
Destroyed by an earthquake in 1766 and rebuilt to a different design

Fatih Camii: Plan. The addition of a half dome to the main dome brings the design closer to the design of Aya Sofya.
Aptullah Kuran

See also view of the new mosque that replaced the original Fatih Camii, and part of the *külliye* on page 126.

Immediately after the conquest, Mehmet II (known as Fatih , meaning Conqueror), adopted Aya Sofya as his imperial mosque (see page 45). In his first years as sultan he reached out to Jewish and Christian communities, appointed the Orthodox and Armenian patriarchs, and employed many Greeks in his administration. Thus he asserted to the citizens of Constantinople that he had assumed the role of Emperor of the Eastern Romans. In 1463, to ensure his enduring status as an Islamic ruler, he began the construction of a mosque and *külliye*, commanding his architect, Atik Sinan, to surpass Aya Sofya. The *külliye*, occupying a large site on the Fourth Hill, was more ambitious than anything

endowed by a previous sultan. It included the provision of four large *medreses*, a hospital and accommodation for travellers. While previous sultans in Bursa and Edirne had built such complexes in a relatively random manner, Mehmet had his laid out to a very formal plan, with its buildings arranged symmetrically on either side of the mosque, on the edges of a broad terrace.

Atik Sinan was probably born a Christian, so it is not surprising that the design of the mosque reflects both Ottoman and Byzantine principles. Many scholars assert that Fatih Camii represents the continuation of Ottoman traditions. They like to see it as an enlargement of Üç Şerefeli Cami in Edirne, with a main dome 26 metres in diameter and the addition of a half dome. Alternatively we can consider it as an adaptation of Aya Sofya with only one half dome. Tursun, Mehmet's court historian, acknowledges Fatih Camii's debt to Aya Sofya. He wrote that the design "not only encompassed all of the arts of Aya Sofya, but moreover incorporated modern features contributing a fresh idiom". Mehmet, however, was not satisfied. The dome did not equal Aya Sofya's 32-metre span.

For the new mosque, rebuilt in 1767, see page 126.

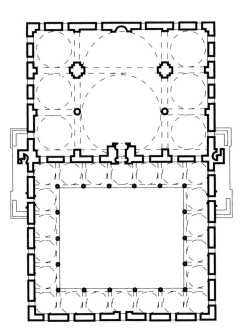

Murat Paşa Camii: Plan.
A simplified mosque of
the Bursa type without
eyvans.
Aptullah Kuran

Murat Paşa, a member of the imperial Byzantine Paleologus family, changed sides at the conquest. He offered his services to Mehmet II and converted to Islam. He soon became a vizier, and finally rose to the elevated position of Viceroy of Europe. However, his life was cut short in a reckless cavalry charge that he led against the advice of an experienced general. His mosque, completed three years earlier, survives to show his ambition as a patron of religious architecture. It stands in a prominent position at the angle of two busy streets in Aksaray. Its thin, alternating bands of red brick and white stone, a common Byzantine technique, stand out in the mainly modern district. Approached through a small garden shaded by plane trees, it is entered through a lofty, five-domed porch with antique columns in red and green marble. Although the columns probably came from a Byzantine building, the capitals are of the *muqarnas* type. Over the door, a fine calligraphic inscription confirms its date.

The two equal domes identify the building as the Bursa type, but it is a step away from the three-*eyvan* type that was common in Bursa, moving closer to a single prayer hall. Unlike the Yeşil Cami in Bursa, for example, the central hall never contained a fountain, while the two spaces on each side for travelling dervishes are closed off, behind doors.

The two domes, as well as the arch between them, are very high, almost giving a sense of a unified space. The first dome is supported on a simplified version of the Turkish band with large triangles, a device not found in any other mosque in Istanbul except for a small version in the narthex of Mahmut Paşa Camii. The second dome is supported on pendentives, ornamented by a *muqarnas* design. Since the intersections of surfaces are picked out in white, both in the Turkish band and the *muqarnas*, their form is easy to see, even in the rather dark interior.

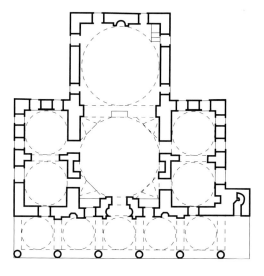

The reign of Mehmet the Conqueror's son, Beyazit II (1481–1512), began with fighting over the succession with his brother Cem. Supported by the Janissaries, he defeated Cem who, after a brief time in Cairo and Rhodes, spent the rest of his days in France and Italy. Beyazit built up the strength of the Ottoman navy, and after capturing Venetian possessions in Morea, made a peace treaty with Venice. Later in life, he devoted himself to the enrichment of Ottoman culture. Beyazit was deposed by his son Selim I in 1512 and died of old age the same year.

This was Beyazit's first major mosque and *külliye*. Built on the outskirts of Edirne, today it still stands isolated among open meadows by the river Tunca. Hayrettin, the architect, provided a very large courtyard, being more than twice the width of the mosque. This was flanked by *tabhanes* where travellers could stay for three days. In addition there was a *medrese*, a soup kitchen, a large hospital with a domed central space, and a *tımarhane* (asylum for the mentally ill). The Ottomans were far more compassionate and more advanced in their treatment of the mentally ill than western European countries. Today the asylum is open to the public as a museum of medical history.

The mosque is a rather plain, domed square, with high walls and pendentives supporting the dome. One can get an excellent view of the whole complex from the dyke running along the river bank. The simple geometry of the main dome, rising from the cubic walls and surrounded by the many small domes of the subsidiary buildings, is striking.

Beyazit II Camii and *külliye*, Edirne, seen in a typical morning mist: The dome of the mosque rises from the plain cubic walls. To the left is the lower dome of the hospital.

Atik Ali Paşa Camii:
View of the dome with
the Süleymaniye Camii
in the background.

Atik Ali Paşa was Chief Vizier for two
periods under Beyazit II. The five-bay
porch of his mosque, unlike that of
Mahmut Paşa Camii, is original, so
we can see how the front of a typical, small, fifteenth-century mosque
looked. With their *muqarnas* capitals, the columns show no traces of
Byzantine influence. The plan is very
close to that of the original Fatih
Camii, though it is smaller in scale.
The central space is similarly expanded by a half dome over the *mihrab*.
The main difference, apart from the
size, is that in this example there are

two domed compartments on either
side of the main space, while in the
old Fatih Camii there were three.
Here the half dome, in its own rectangle, projects from the body of
the mosque, whereas in the Fatih
design the extra domes fill the corners. Unless you go to the somewhat
out-of-the-way Davut Paşa Camii, this
is the only mosque where you will see
muqarnas used in the transition
from the square walls to the curve of
the dome. Here they appear in the
pendentives of the half dome.

Sultan Beyazit II Camii: Compared to the simple hemisphere resting on a cube of Beyazit's mosque in Edirne (see page 55), or Sultan Selim's mosque in Istanbul (see page 60), the outer form here is more complex. The area under the dome opens into secondary spaces around it, while the architect seems to be preoccupied with admitting as much light as possible.

About twelve years after Beyazit II completed his complex in Edirne, he commissioned his architect, Yakup Shah, to build an imperial mosque in Istanbul. In the intervening years he had built an impressive mosque in each of the Anatolian cities of Tokat and Amasya, where he lived for many years as prince-governor. Both mosques were experimental in their

structure. His mosque in Istanbul benefited from these essays in structure and space, but it developed in a new direction. If Fatih Camii is seen as a progression from Üç Şerefeli Cami (page 38), then the design of Beyazit's new mosque followed the structural theme of Aya Sofya (page 42). Yakup Shah extended the space under the central dome by adding two half domes, and creating a long axis. But rather than imitating Aya Sofya, he transformed the character of the interior. Aya Sofya was of course conceived for the Christian liturgy in an imperial context. The central space was reserved for ritual, while the congregation stood in the aisles and galleries. Thus the separation of nave and aisles by four vast piers and the columnar screens that

join them presented no problem. But Yakup Shah, in designing a Muslim prayer hall where the faithful would gather in large numbers for Friday prayers, avoided such hierarchical division. With great engineering skill he reduced the mass of the piers and virtually eliminated the barrier between nave and aisles. He replaced the dense columnar screen of Aya Sofya with two broad arches, and found new ways of admitting light. This is the first imperial mosque with a lofty interior, flooded with light, and surrounded by visually connected subsidiary spaces. Rings of windows penetrate the base of the main dome, and the half domes and the vertical walls on either side contain many windows. In addition the surrounding spaces

are well provided with large openings. In several of the mosques of Bursa the surface decoration of the pendentives provided architectural interest, but here it is achieved by structure and space.

The *avlu* (courtyard) of Sultan Beyazit II Camii is a memorable space. The huge columns with boldly projecting *muqarnas* capitals stand forward boldly against the shade behind; and their shafts of verdantique, porphyry and red granite add to the polychrome effect of the coloured marble voussoirs of the arches. The larger arches on the central axis and the cresting above them emphasise the entrances. Note the ingenious manner in which voussoirs over the portals interlock.

right
Sultan Beyazit II Camii:
Plan, derived from
that of Aya Sofya. The
harmony of the plan is
based on a rigorous
system of proportions.
Both the courtyard and
the prayer hall occupy a
perfect square. The
prayer hall is planned
on sixteen equal
squares, of which four
are covered by the
central dome.
Cornelius Gurlitt

opposite
Sultan Beyazit II Camii:
View from the north-
east corner into the
dome and southern half
dome. See also interior
view on page 50.

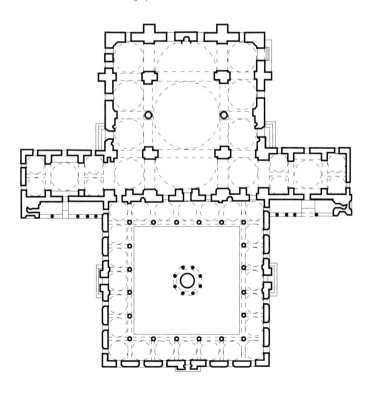

Sultan Selim Camii:
Interior. The penden-
tives of the shallow
dome rise from a point
not far above the floor.
Note the fine *minber*.

It is unclear whether or not Selim began this mosque himself, but it was certainly completed by his son Süleyman two years after his death. Selim the Grim, as he was known, fought to gain the Ottoman throne in 1511. He forced his father Beyazit II to abdicate and, to eliminate other contenders, killed his elder brother and four nephews. He was a formidable warrior, whose defeat of the Mamluk State added Syria, Egypt and Arabia to the empire. The conquest of Arabia was particularly significant, because it made him the protector of the holy cities of Mecca and Medina, and therefore the caliph of all Muslims. He won an important victory at Çaldıran in eastern Anatolia in 1514 over the Safavid Shah Ismail, and pressed on to Tabriz. Neither Selim nor his successors succeeded in bringing Persia into the empire, but his conquest of Tabriz had a profound effect on architecture and decorative art in Turkey. He brought many fine craftsmen from there to work in Istanbul. The result was a Persian influence on design and decoration. While, at first, Selim was admired by his troops for his courage, his habit of executing generals and officials who had offended him soon struck fear in the hearts of those around him. Despite his brutal thirst for power, Selim wrote poetry in the Persian language. In 1520 he died while planning an attack, possibly aimed at the island stronghold of Rhodes.

Selim's son Süleyman behaved magnanimously on his succession. He was determined to be just and redressed some of his father's harsher measures. European leaders looked hopefully to the new, young sultan, believing that he might seek peace with Christendom. However, he launched a campaign against Hungary the very next year, and took Belgrade after a short siege. It was after his triumphant return from that campaign, knowing that his father would have approved of his military success, that he completed Sultan Selim Camii in his honour. It stands on the edge of Fifth Hill on a terrace that juts out from the steep slope above Fener and can easily be seen from Galata and the Golden Horn. Unless you climb up steep streets through a decayed neighbourhood, you will approach from the top of the hill and view the mosque across the huge sunken area that was once the Byzantine cistern of Aspar.

Sultan Selim Camii is the simplest imperial mosque in Istanbul, consisting of a well-proportioned court and a single square prayer hall covered by a shallow dome 24.5 metres wide. In its juxtaposition of cubic and rounded forms, without the complication of half domes, it is rather similar to the Beyazit II Camii in Edirne. The interior proportions are unusual in Istanbul, where interiors tend to soar skywards. As was common in early Ottoman mosques,

Sultan Selim Camii: Exterior. This mosque retains the simplicity typical of early Ottoman designs.

the pendentives spring from a point no higher than the top of the *mihrab*. Without the elaborately painted decorations found in so many mosques, the interior seems austere. However, there is richness in the detail, as well as evidence of Persian craftsmanship. The lunettes (upper parts) of the arches over the lower windows, both in the southeast arcade of the court and the interior, are decorated with delicately patterned İznik tiles. These were made during the earliest period of İznik ceramics by the "cuerda seca" technique, in which the colours of the glaze were separated with a thin line of dry material before firing (see page 89). The result is exceptional clarity of the colours. The painted, wooden ceiling under the sultan's lodge, predominantly in red and gold, is exquisite. There are also fine panels of İznik tiles on either side of the entry to Selim's tomb in the garden behind the mosque, where he was buried in solitary state. Imagine the gravity of those occasions when Süleyman visited this tomb (and the tombs of his grandfather Beyazit and Mehmet the Conqueror, built beside their mosques), before leaving with his army on military campaigns, as if to win encouragement for his venture.

An attractive feature of the precinct is the terrace, shaded by old trees and arranged with little tables, where neighbourhood families often relax and picnic. The view over the Golden Horn from this high vantage point is superb.

Sultan Selim's tomb:
One of two exquisite
panels of İznik tiles
flanking the entrance.

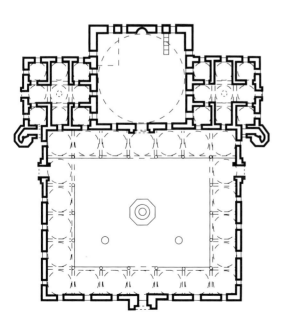

above
Sultan Selim Camii:
Early İznik tiles in a
lunette over a window
of the courtyard.

left
Sultan Selim Camii:
Plan. The prayer hall is
almost a cube, covered
by a hemisphere. The
nine small domed
spaces contained in a
square on each side of
the mosque provided
accommodation for
travelling dervishes.

MOSQUES OF THE CLASSICAL PERIOD
BY SINAN THE GREAT

Mimar Sinan: Chief Architect of Süleyman the Magnificent

While Italian Renaissance architects from Brunelleschi to Michelangelo created their masterly designs for large domed churches, an equally momentous development took place in the Ottoman Empire. Mimar Sinan, the Chief Architect to three Sultans from 1538 to 1588, experimented boldly with structure, space and light in a vast array of domed mosques. On one hand the Italian architects conceived new types of design in response to the demands of Christianity, and to the architectural theory of humanist scholars; on the other, Sinan observed traditional principles of Islamic architecture, and served the needs of his clients. With a genius for structural design, he oversaw a great metamorphosis of the mosque and set the course for the design of mosques for centuries to come. Both Italian and Ottoman architects absorbed Roman and Byzantine influences, but they interpreted them in entirely different ways.

Sinan's mosques offer enormous scope for study because he and his assistants completed so many of them. While no Italian architect built more than a few domed structures, Sinan is credited with over a hundred, including eighteen in Istanbul alone. While St. Peter's took almost 90 years to build, with several changes of architect, the great Süleymaniye mosque was completed in only seven years. Sinan's works are spread from the Balkans, through Anatolia to Damascus, Baghdad and Jerusalem. He not only experimented vigorously with alternative schemes, but also continued to refine his details. His early mosques built around 1540 show expertise; over the next decades he progressed towards mastery of his profession, reaching a peak in 1570 with the creation of the Selimiye Camii at Edirne. Since he held the position of Chief of Architects for 50 years his opportunities were unparalleled in architectural history.

The Life of Sinan

Sinan was born a Christian, probably Greek or Armenian, between 1489 and 1491 in a village near Kayseri in central Anatolia. In about 1514 he was recruited by the *devşirme*, an organisation that selected young Christian men to serve the Sultan. They were converted to Islam and, although they were technically slaves, they had the opportunity to progress in the palace service or in the Janissary Corps, an elite wing of the Ottoman army. Sinan was enrolled, first as a novice and then into the Janissaries, and was taught the trade of carpentry, at which he excelled. He participated in many military campaigns, ranging from Central Europe to Iran and Iraq, and received regular promotions. In his role of military engineer he oversaw the building of fortifications, ships and bridges, making his reputation most decisively when he constructed a bridge for the movement of troops over the River Pruth in Moldavia in just a few days

During his extensive travels for military purposes he must have seen fine examples of the architecture of several civilisations, and observed their principles and aesthetic qualities. On the basis of his exceptional talents and flair for organisation, he was appointed chief architect to the Sultan in 1538. From then until his death at the age of about 90 he was responsible, with the assistance of a corps of architects, for the design and construction of over

400 buildings. Sinan was fortunate to begin his career during the illustrious reign of Süleyman I, known to Europeans as Süleyman the Magnificent and to Muslims as Süleyman the Lawgiver. The Sultan's many military campaigns, in which he personally led his troops in battle, greatly expanded his empire and his wealth. He was an outstanding patron of the arts, and presided over a golden age for architecture.

Sinan's Italian contemporary Michelangelo designed one great domed church, St. Peter's, Rome, but he did not live to see it finished. Sinan was responsible for many domed mosques and had time to apply what he learned from each project to future designs. A visit to a dozen of his most ambitious mosques reveals the breadth of his experiments with a variety of structural forms and spatial types. Modifying and refining his designs in the light of experience, he was able to push the boundaries of architecture and create soaring spaces flooded with light. However, Sinan was not solely concerned with the satisfaction of his own artistic ambitions. He was deeply committed to Islam, and was devoted to the service of his patrons.

Gülru Necipoğlu, in her book *The Age of Sinan*, argues that Sinan was not "a 'Turkish Michelangelo' driven solely by an insatiable urge for artistic experimentation". Rather, she demonstrates that "Sinan's rich variety of mosque designs sprang from a process of negotiation between the architect and his elite patrons, both men and women". His work cannot be discussed only in formal terms, but must be considered in the context of his age.

Mihrimah Sultan Camii, Edirnekapı: One of Sinan's dynamic variations on domed interior space.

above:
Haseki Camii: Aerial view. Mosque with twin domes (top centre), the original *külliye* (below left), and additional charitable foundations (top left and lower right).
Reha Günay

below:
Haseki Camii: Section. The square of the walls is converted to a circle by means of squinches in the form of scallop shells.
Cornelius Gurlitt

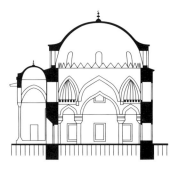

This, Sinan's first mosque, was built by Süleyman for his wife, Haseki Hürrem, known in the West as Roxelana. She was probably the daughter of an Orthodox priest of Ukranian descent and was brought to the harem after being captured on a raid in Poland. Süleyman, departing from Ottoman custom, had a passionate monogamous relationship with her. The letters and poetry written during military campaigns reveal the sensitive nature of this powerful warrior, and show that he was deeply in love with her. As the first sultan to formalise marriage with his favourite, Süleyman allowed Hürrem to become politically powerful. Court protocol did not permit the sultan's concubines to bear more than one son, but Hürrem presented him with four: Abdullah, who died in infancy, Mehmet, Selim and Beyazit, as well as beloved daughter Mihrimah. Haseki Camii was the first to be endowed by a sultan's wife or concubine. Hürrem, though generally unpopular, was known for her compassion for the poor. Desiring to gain favour with the people, and hoping to ensure the succession of her own son to the throne, she commissioned Sinan to include in the complex a *medrese* and a *mekteb* (school for young boys), a school and a hospice. Thus she was patron of a large and important *külliye*, which acted as the nucleus of an urban neighbourhood.

The mosque consisted of a single square, covered with a dome 11.3 metres in diameter. The transition from the square walls to the circle is made by eight slightly pointed arches forming an octagon. The four that span across the corners of the square to act as squinches are grooved like scallop shells, in a manner very similar to the smaller domes of the Üç Şerefeli Cami in Edirne (see page 38). The intermediate arches are pierced by windows. In 1612 the mosque was enlarged by opening the eastern wall and adding a second, identical domed space.

21 MİHRİMAH SULTAN CAMİİ (Itinerary D)
(Iskele Camii)
Üsküdar, 1543/44–48

Süleyman's daughter Mihrimah commissioned this mosque, shortly after her marriage to the grand vizier Rüstem Paşa. It is also known as the Iskele Camii (ferry landing mosque). It continues the tradition followed by Hürrem of patronage by female members of the royal household. Its two minarets, normally proclaiming a sultan's mosque, show the favour that her father bestowed on her. As her mother's *külliye* had done previously, it included a *medrese* and a *mekteb*, which both survive. Today the mosque stands well back from the waterfront at Üsküdar, on the Asian side of the Bosphorus, but when it was first built the water came close to its wall. This explains the height of the terrace on which it stands and the rather compressed plan, imposed by the narrowness of the site between the shore and the steep hill behind it. There was no room for a courtyard, but Sinan used his ingenuity to create a calm transitional space between the urban bustle of Üsküdar and the interior of the mosque. He gave it the usual portico with five domes and on three sides of that he placed a broad, low-pitched roof that slopes down to protect an outer porch. This device, which appears on several of his later mosques, seems to be one of Sinan's many architectural innovations. From the waterfront one sees not a towering façade, rising up to the dome in a

Mihrimah Sultan Camii: Exterior from the south-east. Two of the three half domes can be seen swelling out below the main dome.

flamboyant manner, but the long, low, horizontal lines of the porch roof and the deep shade between the stone wall of the terrace. The central part of this roof, extending forwards to cover the fountain, contributes to the human scale of the design. This sheltering roof finds a modern counterpart in the low-pitched, hipped roofs of Frank Lloyd Wright's "Prairie Houses" in which the architect sought to combine a symbol of protection and integration with the land.

You will enter up a simple flight of steps on the west side, near the fine

Baroque fountain of Ahmet III (1726) at street level, and immediately find shade under the roof of the outer porch. The light here is subdued, and despite the superb view across the Bosphorus, the outer arcade and surrounding trees create a sense of enclosure to the sacred precinct. The polygonal marble fountain shines in the brighter light outside, and gives a reminder of religious duty. Except for a passage leading to the central portal, the floor of the inner porch is raised up, to make additional space for prayer. Although this is seen to be

the latecomers' porch, it is also used between prayer times. There are two wall niches acting as exterior *mihrabs*.

On entering the mosque, you will look up to see a central dome supported on plain columns and three half domes. Fatih Camii had one half dome over the *mihrab*; Beyazit II Camii had two, extending the central space along the central axis, in the manner of Hagia Sophia. Sinan, in his first use of this element, chose to widen the interior with lateral half domes as well as one opposite the entrance.

If he had wished to include a fourth to perfect the symmetry, the narrowness of the site discouraged it. The result is that the space feels somewhat constricted and, because of the porch, it is rather dark. However, the central dome, with three half domes billowing out around it, is an inspiring sight and a promise of things to come in the architect's repertoire.

A passage at the eastern end of the porch leads to the entrance of the *medrese*, which is now a health clinic. The courtyard is covered over in a rather curious way using mirror glass, but the elegant arcades survive and you can imagine its former character as a religious school. The *mekteb* still stands on the hill behind the mosque. The *hamam* (bath) of Roxelana, also by Sinan, still stands too.

Completion of Mihrimah Sultan Camii was delayed when Süleyman directed Sinan to begin work on Şehzade Camii. Although his daughter's project was begun at least a year earlier, the two were finished in the same year.

Mihrimah Sultan Camii: View of the broad double porch. Such porches are often used by latecomers at prayer times.

opposite
Şehzade Camii: Below
the main dome, one of
the four half domes
is flanked by two
weight towers.

below
Şehzade Camii: The
plan and section show
Sinan's use of pure
geometry to achieve
ideal form.
Aptullah Kuran

In 1543, Süleyman was grief stricken when Hürrem's eldest son Şehzade (Prince) Mehmet died of smallpox at the age of 21. Süleyman received the news as he returned from a victorious campaign. Mourning beside the coffin for three days before allowing burial, he then commanded Sinan to build a magnificent mosque to commemorate the prince. The architect responded with a design that outshone the other sultans' mosques in the city. His solution was to complete the evolution he had begun in

Mihrimah Sultan Camii in Üsküdar (page 67) and add a fourth half dome, thus making the structure completely symmetrical on both axes. He probably reflected on the structural inconsistency at Aya Sofya, where the dome is supported with buttresses on two sides and half domes on the other two. In his design for Şehzade Camii he equalised the forces in a logical way by placing half domes all around. But perhaps Sinan's most important goal was to achieve unity of form. Architects and theorists of the Italian Renaissance believed that pure geometric forms such as the circle, the square and the octagon were ideal for church plans because they reflected the perfection of God. Although no theoretical writings by Islamic scholars make the same case, it is clear that Sinan and his predecessors honoured God with designs based on mathematical harmony. The 19-metre dome, poised over the centre of a square, can be interpreted as a symbol of the heavens and of spiritual unity under God. The plan of the central part of the mosque is almost identical, in its geometrical basis, to the church of Santa Maria della Consolazione at Todi, in Italy. For all their theoretical perfection, centralised churches proved unsuitable for the Catholic liturgy, and few were built. On the other hand, Sinan's design for Şehzade Camii was copied in thousands of mosques all over Turkey and other parts of the Islamic world – a broad space under a dome, expanding equally on all sides, makes an excellent Muslim prayer hall.

Şehzade Camii is on the north side of the Şehzadebaşı Caddesi, behind a high stone wall. Designed by Sinan, the *türbes* (tombs) of Şehzade

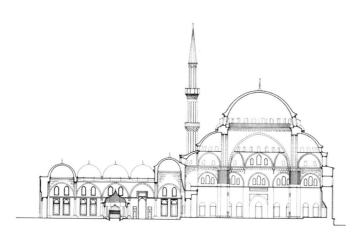

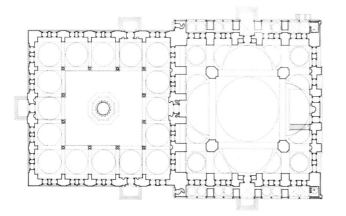

Mehmet and two of Süleyman's grand viziers (Rüstem Paşa and Ibrahim Paşa) are visible behind the eastern end of the wall. These richly tiled tombs are not open to visitors, but you can appreciate them as part of the historical context of Süleyman's reign. Looking up, above the square top of the walls, you will see the small domes in the corners and the half domes clustering around the high, central hemisphere. Between them, slim cylindrical towers, also capped with cupolas, rise as high as the windows in the drum of the main dome. These are weight towers, that stand directly above the four main structural piers inside. Their purpose is to counteract the immense outward thrust of the dome by exerting a powerful down-

ward force. All these elements create a dynamic composition as they step up gradually from the cubic upper walls to the crown of the dome. The mass of the wall is broken down into smaller elements that conceal the massive buttresses. Sinan created lively rhythms by alternating solid piers and slender columns in the front arcade of the porch. The tall narrow arches, casting deep shadows, contrast with the broader arches of the windows on the floor above.

It is interesting to compare this façade with that of a typical Italian Renaissance church. The latter would be articulated with classical columns or pilasters and crowned by a pediment. The façade of Şehzade Camii makes no such symbolic reference to an ancient tradition; rather

it reflects the interior. Sinan placed the openings so that light floods into the prayer hall, wherever the structure allows.

Before entering the mosque, walk to the left, around the wall of the courtyard. You will see the main portal rising through two stories and terminating above the roofline. Note the elegant details and the contrast between the plain frame of the portal and the rich *muqarnas* vault over the recess. If this portal is open, enter through the court and enjoy the human scale of the arcade.

Once inside, you will appreciate how Sinan opened up the interior. The tall, slender piers offer little obstruction. The pendentives make a simple transition to the dome. Unlike Beyazit II Camii, with its long axis between two half domes in the manner of Aya Sofya, the central space in Şehzade Camii expands in four directions. Beyazit's architect Yakup Shah had avoided some of the complexity of Aya Sofya by eliminating exedrae flanking the apse, but here Sinan played variations on the Byzantine theme, and introduced his own elaboration. He supported each of the half domes on three equal arches – a central one over a vertical wall, flanked by two that open into smaller half domes. These span the corners like squinches, thus making the transition from rectangle to half circle. On the tier below, three smaller arches follow the outline of the rectangle. The result is a structure that combines complexity and consistency. He has approached the richness of Aya Sofya, but in a more rational

manner. In the entire plan there is a progression from 24 arches in the lowest tier to twelve on the next, and from there to the four that support the central dome. The massive weight of the dome is distributed between a multitude of structural supports, and brought gracefully to the foundations.

Sinan created a duality between the static structure of the four massive piers and arches in the centre and the flowing forms of smaller arches around them. Copious, diffused light flows into the interior through small windows in the bases of the domes and half domes, as well as in the vertical walls. It is clear that Sinan admired Aya Sofya but was not content to imitate it. He reinterpreted its design for Islamic worship and the desires of his own age.

opposite
Şehzade Camii: The elaborate system of support for the dome with piers, arches and half domes.

below
Şehzade Camii: South façade. See also the interior view on page 15.

opposite
Süleymaniye Camii:
The light, spacious interior of the prayer hall.

Below
Süleymaniye Camii:
Night view from the
Golden Horn. Below it
lie the Yeni Valide Cami
and, to the right, the
Rüstem Paşa Camii.

In the thirtieth year of his reign, Süleyman embarked on his greatest building project, Süleymaniye Camii. Up to this time his most important religious endowment had been the Şehzade Camii, built in honour of his dead son. Now, at the age of 55, it was time for him to think of his own memorial on the skyline of the city and his own rewards in paradise. More than a thousand years before, Justinian had claimed to surpass Soloman by building Aya Sofya. Süleyman shared the same name as the biblical king and saw himself as his heir. The sultan was also making a political statement about his role as a world potentate. In 1547, in a letter to the Holy Roman Emperor, Charles V, Süleyman had addressed Charles as "King of the province of Spain". He styled himself as the emperor "who

commands the caesars of the era and crowns the emperors of the world". Indeed, as a descendant of Mehmet II, conqueror of Constantinople, he claimed to be the inheritor of the Roman Empire. He expressed his ambition with the statement: "When the Angel Gabriel shakes the world only [my works] will survive."

Mimar Sinan's duty as architect was to proclaim the sultan's magnificence and power in solid stone and overwhelming interior space. He was commissioned to place the mosque at the heart of an educational complex, with no less than seven *medreses*, that would flourish as Istanbul's intellectual centre. No doubt the sultan took a keen interest in the design and in the progress of the construction. He possessed artistic interests and sensibilities. As a

young man he had learned the art of making jewelry and had experienced the joy of artistic creation. He was also an accomplished poet. Throughout his reign he was a discriminating patron of the arts with a corps of architects and hundreds of skilled artisans under his command.

The irregular topography was a challenge to Sinan. The sloping terrain was suitable for the terraced gardens of the old palace, but the architect wanted the mosque to rise majestically from a broad, level platform. On the two sides where the ground fell away, he bolstered the edge of the terrace with buildings at a lower level, but still needed thousands of ox carts of fill to bring the ground up to the desired height. He was unable to arrange the buildings of the *külliye* as formally as those of the Fatih complex, but he could still plan the mosque with rigorous symmetry. A powerful axis runs from the northwest entrance, through the impressive main portal of the courtyard, into the mosque interior and to the *mihrab* on the southeast side. It then continues through the centre of the sultan's *türbe* and the *dar-ül-kurra* (house for the readers of the *Qur'an*). This is, of course, the *qibla* axis, leading straight to Mecca.

Süleyman's exalted status is expressed in the four tall minarets at the corners of the court. Only a sultan's mosque could be graced with more than one minaret. Süleyman had already departed from custom when he ordered a minaret with more than one gallery for the Şehzade Camii, and two minarets for Mihrimah; in his own mosque he exceeded any precedent, by erecting four beautifully proportioned minarets. The pair at the eastern end of the court were provided with two

Sinan brought variety into the composition by, on the one hand, organising its mass harmoniously within the outline of a pyramid to create stability; and on the other hand, enlivening it with a rhythmic treatment of its minor elements. The small domes over the aisle alternate in size, with larger ones in the corners and the centre. The domes capping the buttresses and weight towers add to the variety. Beneath them the arches in the upper walls follow the same alternating rhythm. One interesting aspect of the treatment of the façades is the lower story of the walls. By fronting them with open arcades he created a more human scale. The two-tiered arcades between the buttresses serve no functional purpose (the galleries behind them are virtually inaccessible), but the deep shade they create and their smaller structural elements mediate with the massiveness of the buttresses. This device is particularly appropriate because along the base of the wall are the many water taps for ablutions. The faithful are even sheltered by a projecting roof as they sit on marble benches to wash before prayer.

Walk along this wall and enter through the courtyard. While still outside, it is easy to imagine the splendour of the processions circumambulating the mosque on the many occasions when Süleyman attended Friday prayers, and as you enter the spacious and elegant court consider its suitability for rituals of pomp and piety. Some of the paving stones actually mark the places where particular dignitaries stood. The surrounding arcades are formed with seven arches on each side, supported on shafts of pink porphyry, red granite and white marble,

galleries each, while the higher ones abutting the wall of the mosque display three galleries, a number only seen previously in the Üç Şerefeli Cami in Edirne.

As the mosque rises in a series of steps to the crown of the dome, the exterior proclaims the interior. It is clear, in the manner of a Gothic cathedral, how the various elements interact to create a vast, well-lit interior. You can easily see the structural skeleton made up of the massive buttresses projecting from the lower walls, the great arch that springs from the interior piers to support the

dome, the weight towers flanking the arch that stand directly above the piers to counteract the outward thrust of the dome, and the smaller buttresses around the drum of the dome that also help to contain its forces. To either side, the half domes that elongate the interior space are just visible. Equally obvious is the means by which the huge prayer hall is flooded with daylight. The broad arches in the lower walls contain windows to light the aisles. Twenty-two openings penetrate the great arch, and a ring of windows in the drum of the dome focus light on the centre.

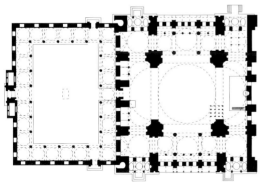

opposite
Süleymaniye Camii:
Aerial view showing the
formal, axial layout of
the mosque within its
külliye.
Reha Günay

left
Süleymaniye Camii:
Plan. The structural
concept is similar
to that of Aya Sofya,
but Sinan has reduced
the mass of the
supports to make a
spacious prayer hall.
Cornelius Gurlitt

above
Süleymaniye Camii:
View with the Golden
Horn in the distance.
The outer form reflects
the structural system
and interior space.

brought from the royal box of the Byzantine Hippodrome. The stalactite capitals, however, are distinctly Ottoman in design. To add to the richness, the arches are built of alternating red and white stone. As is usual, the central arches on the main axis are wider to emphasise the entrance. Before passing into the interior, be sure to look up at the central dome of the arcade, slightly higher than the others and supported on stalactite consoles.

Sinan, possibly at the request of the sultan, reverted to the structural scheme of a central dome and two half domes that is the basis of Aya Sofya. However, Süleymaniye Camii possesses its own architectural identity, quite distinct from its Byzantine predecessor. Above all, Sinan created the most open interior possible, and broke down the barrier between central and surrounding spaces. Although he emphasised the main north–south axis to the *mihrab*, he also opened up the east–west axis on which many rows of the faithful prostrate themselves in prayer. Where the nave is separated from the aisles and galleries by massive piers and a screen of five arches in Aya Sofya, Sinan's piers are comparatively slender, and only two columns carrying three arches separate the aisles from the central space. The columns of porphyry from the Roman city of Baalbek in Syria remind us of the resources that Süleyman had at his command. Other columns were brought from far away Alexandria. The galleries, independently supported on marble columns, are set back against the outer walls and have little impact on the space of the prayer hall.

The vast scale of Süleymaniye Camii can be somewhat overwhelming, but there is plenty of detail to enjoy. Sinan aimed to create beauty through perfection of form rather than lavish decoration. Süleyman had been ostentatious during the early years of his reign, but later his dress and his way of life had become more ascetic. Therefore the ornament was rather restrained. Notice, both on the exterior and the interior, the refinement and subtlety of the mouldings around the doors, windows and niches. There is no elaboration for its own sake; the architect's simple aim is to turn corners gracefully. The grey stone *mihrab* is quite sober, but a closer look at the wall reveals exquisite tiling with blossoming trees and birds on the wall beside it. This was the first example of tiles applied over such a wide area. Elsewhere tiles are used sparingly, but they are of the highest quality and provide touches of colour here and there. They are of a new type which was being developed at İznik, where deep blue, green and red stand out against a white background. The beautifully carved *minber*, of Marmara marble, is surprisingly plain. Inscriptions over doorways picked out in gold, over courtyard windows in blue and white tiles, and painted in the dome are all excellent examples of the calligrapher's art. They are probably the work of Çerkes Hasan Çelebi. The inscription from the *Qur'an*, in the centre of the dome, begins: "God is the light of the heavens and the earth." The roundels in the pendentives, radiating from a hub rather like Gothic rose windows, contain Arabic script dynamically integrated with geometric abstraction. The brilliantly colourful glass was made by a craftsman known as Ibrahim the Drunkard. The plaster tracery that holds it in place has been restored, but the glass is mostly original.

When you exit the mosque, take a few steps to the right. Just above eye level on the wall beside you is a sundial. Its incised lines have almost eroded away, but two bronze elements project from the wall to cast a shadow (see page 81). On turning back to the left you will reach a gate into the walled cemetery on the left. Here are the tombs of Süleyman, who died in 1566, and his wife Hürrem, who died before him in 1558. Both are lined with outstanding İznik tiles and Süleyman's, the larger of the two, has a marvellous painted ceiling. Clearly, the erection of the tomb was a key part of the sultan's grand design. Visible from the Golden Horn and Galata, it is probably the most prominent tomb in Istanbul.

Having visited the mosque and tombs, it is time to consider their surroundings. Although the street to the southwest is mainly given over to tourist activities, one can get an idea of the original *külliye*. On the southwest side, behind the shops and cafés, are two buildings constructed as schools of Islamic law. They are now occupied by the Süleymaniye library where an important collection of manuscripts is available to scholars. Behind the northern end of the row of shops was a medical college, and in the corner a hospital. At the end of the street you will find steps down into a café in a sunken courtyard. Turning right onto Şifahane Sokağı you will come to the entrance of the kitchen that fed students at the *medreses*, the poor, and all those who worked in the mosque and the *külliye*. Today this is a restaurant specialising in traditional Turkish dishes.

Next is the former Caravanserai, which would once have teemed with travellers and their animals. Mimar Sinan's tomb can be seen by turning right at the next corner, and beyond his tomb are the walls of two further *medreses*.

Return through the gate on the main axis of the mosque. Although the main portal to the courtyard on this axis is not usually open, it is worth standing at the gate in the outer wall that aligns with it to sense the strength of the symmetry. From here you will be aware that the walls of the precinct, to your right, and the edge of the terrace overlooking the Golden Horn, to your left, are equidistant from the walls of the mosque. Such geometrical order reinforces the serene dominance of the mosque, which appears as stable as a pyramid as it rises from its perfect pedestal. From this position the dome is scarcely visible. It is concealed behind the high and rather plain wall in which the tall, narrow

portal is incised. You will see the 56-metre-high minarets, each with two balconies, flanking the façade, and beyond them, the taller three-balconied minarets rising from the corners of the mosque to a height of 76 metres. The upper story above the portal was the house of the sultan's astronomer, a very important person in Süleyman's time. Walking out onto the terrace on the left, you can see the whole mosque again and enjoy one of the greatest urban experiences of Europe. On one side, the mosque towers above you; on the other you can see across the Golden Horn to Galata, and over the Bosphorus to Asia.

Süleymaniye Camii: View into the 26-metre dome and southern half dome. The many-windowed walls under the great eastern and western arches admit copious light.

Islamic Astronomy and Sundials

During the period known in Europe as the Dark Ages, astronomers and mathematicians in the Islamic world were far ahead of their Christian contemporaries. Before the time of Muhammad, Arabs were already wise observers of the skies, but with the advent of Islam the need arose to determine prayer times accurately and to establish the direction to Mecca from every city. In the eighth and ninth centuries, scholars were absorbing and translating astronomical works in Sanskrit, Pahlavi, Greek and Syriac. They drew on the geography and other works of the Greco-Egyptian mathematician Ptolemy, adapting his principles and methods to their needs. Thus they followed and even improved on Hellenistic, Iranian and Indian traditions of mathematical astronomy. Using such tools as the astrolabe and trigonometry, their advances in spherical astronomy enabled them to prepare countless tables to establish the direction of Mecca and prayer times in different locations. By the fifteenth century, astronomers were attached to major mosques in Ottoman Turkey and Mamluk Egypt. At Süleymaniye Camii the astronomer was honoured with an apartment over the main entrance on the northwest side.

In early times, the first prayer of the day was called by the *müezzin* at the moment at which there was enough light to distinguish a black thread and a white thread from each other. At noon, the shortest shadow cast by a vertical rod signalled the time of prayer. These methods were superceded by the use of sundials. First created in Egypt by 1500 BCE, they were further developed during the Seljuk era, and by the fifteenth century were part of most Ottoman mosques. While some were horizontal, like those seen in Europe, the majority were aligned vertically on walls. In many cases, one on the south wall was used to give the time of morning and noon prayers, while another on the west side established the later prayer times. Because the length of the day varies with the seasons, the design of these sundials was complicated and they do not all follow the same pattern. They represent varied attempts to make it possible for mosque officials to fix prayer times at any stage of the year.

Superceded by clocks, most of the sundials disappeared. Often the "gnomons" (the metal rods projecting from the wall to cast a shadow) were pulled out, and the lines incised on the stone walls became eroded. However, some can still be found, often as a faint pattern of lines below the small hole that once held the gnomons. The best places to see them are at the Fatih, Sultan Selim, Beyazit II, Mihrimah Sultan in Üsküdar, Süleymaniye, Yeni Valide in Eminönü, and Laleli mosques.

opposite
Süleymaniye Camii:
The southwest wall.
The arcades and
overhanging roofs
create a human scale.
At the foot of the wall
are white marble seats
and water taps for
ablutions.

Kara Ahmet Paşa Camii: Sinan's structural virtuosity is evident in this dome on hexagonal supports.

While Sinan Paşa Camii (opposite) could be considered to be merely a reworking of Üç Şerefeli Cami (page 38), Kara Ahmet Paşa Camii shows a flourishing of the architect's originality and aesthetic sense. It is the first of a series of designs in which he played with variations on the hexagonal theme. The arches supporting the dome spring from six freestanding columns, giving the interior a structural lightness that he had never achieved before. The conches behind the lateral arches billow out on either side of the central space, while openings in the conches reveal galleries beyond. Small squinches with shell designs embellish the corners of the conches. Light pours in through unusually large windows in the base of the dome and on all sides at a lower level.

A novel feature of the interior is that of the main columns, which give the impression of holding up the dome with their slender shafts and boldly projecting capitals. Actually the solid walls close behind them are carrying the load. This device was used by the Romans in interiors such as the Basilica of Constantine. Fourteen years later, in Selimiye Camii in Edirne, Sinan was to advance to a point where he could have eight slender piers standing further out from the surrounding walls to carry the dome's magnificent canopy. Kara Ahmet Paşa Camii seems to take a step towards that structural solution.

The approach to the mosque is through an attractive courtyard, surrounded by the cells and classroom of a *medrese*. İznik tiles in the lunettes over the courtyard doors and windows are exceptionally fine.

Kara Ahmet Paşa took over as grand vizier from Rüstem Paşa in 1553, after Rüstem Paşa was dismissed from office in disgrace (see page 84). But Kara Ahmet was to suffer a worse fate than Rüstem, as he was executed two years later. Ahmet's mosque and tomb, which stand inside the Theodosian walls north of Topkapı Gate, were finished after his death.

25 SİNAN PAŞA CAMİİ (Itinerary G)
Beşiktaş 1554–55/56

Sinan Paşa Camii: The complex interior shows the influence of the Üç Şerefeli Cami (see page 38).

Sinan Paşa was Grand Admiral of the Ottoman navy and brother of the powerful grand vizier, Rüstem Paşa. His mosque stands just opposite the Beşiktaş ferry terminal and Maritime Museum. Its solid walls, with polychrome bands of red brick and limestone, afford some protection from the roaring traffic. Fortunately the entrance is at the back, off a more peaceful courtyard. The design is interesting because Sinan chose to revisit the concept of Üç Şerefeli Cami in Edirne (see page 38). As he was responsible for the upkeep of mosques throughout the empire, Sinan may have been involved with restoration at the Üç Şerefeli Cami. His unwillingness to dismiss it as something of the past suggests a love for his architectural heritage and a fascination with this pivotal design. It also reinforces the fact that Sinan wanted to make each of his mosques in the capital unique. He achieved some refinements in the proportions, making the two freestanding columns more elegant and raising the dome a little higher. He has been accused of failure to solve the problem of the little domed triangles between the large and small domes, and thus detracting from the unity of the space, but these features are intriguing. The rather bare narthex, which seems unworthy of a Sinan mosque, is in fact a later addition which involved the enclosure of the original latecomers' porch to accommodate more worshippers.

As has already been seen, Ottoman mosques, whether built by sultans or grand viziers, demonstrate the status of their patrons. They also give a key to the distinctive capabilities of state-supported workshops at the time when they were endowed. Nowhere is this more obvious than Rüstem Paşa Camii. It expresses Rüstem's ambition and his obsession with his own success. As grand vizier he encouraged development of the luxury textile and ceramic industries, and it seems that his own personal taste was highly influential on the designers and craftsmen of his day. He controlled many of the empire's activities and enterprises and put the finances of the Ottoman state in good order. Meanwhile he amassed great personal wealth,

much of which he spent on charitable foundations. The husband of Mihrimah, Süleyman's daughter, he possessed exceptional power. However, in 1553 he was implicated in a plot devised by the sultan's wife Hürrem to ensure the succession of her son Selim (by murdering his elder brother Mustafa). When the prince was strangled during a campaign in Persia, the Janissaries and many others were outraged. He was capable and popular, while Selim was generally despised. To assuage public anger, Süleyman stripped Rüstem of his positions as general and grand vizier. Two years later, when the furore had died down, Rüstem resumed his former roles.

It was not until after Rüstem's death that his mosque was built. He

Rüstem Paşa Camii: The dome rises high above the commercial district of Eminönü. The minarets of Süleymaniye Camii are visible in the background.

Rüstem Paşa Camii:
Detail of the transition
between piers, arches
and dome.

probably acquired the site and had
begun planning the mosque during
his second term of office, but it was
his widow Mihrimah who brought
the project to fruition. It seems likely
that it was she who demanded the
luxuriously tiled interior.

Despite his power and wealth,
there were limits to what could be
built in Rüstem's name. Only a sultan could build more than one
minaret, and a very large dome
would have suggested arrogant
competition with the sultan. Sinan
compensated for the modest span of
the dome by making it very high,
and he gave the interior an unprece-
dented richness by lining it, up to
the base of the dome, with İznik
tiles. Rüstem made sure that the
mosque would produce income in
perpetuity, so that its maintenance
would not be a drain on his purse. To
that end he planned it in a market
area between the port on the Golden

Horn and the Grand Bazaar. It is
raised up above a full story of shops
and *hans*, whose rents provided a
substantial endowment. Although
the dome of the mosque is easily visible from the Galata Bridge and the
shore of Eminönü, it is hard to find
when one is close to it. But signs in
the passages beneath show the way
to steps leading up to it, and an
arcade in front of its elevated porch
can be seen from Uzunçarşı Caddesi,
a little west of the bridge.

If a place in paradise is guaranteed
to the builders of truly exquisite
mosques, we can be sure that
Rüstem Paşa, for all the controversy
that surrounds him, is well treated
in the afterlife. The interior of his
prayer hall may come as close as
any to an image of paradise. This is
Sinan's first octagonal mosque, and
it can be seen as a step on the way to
his greatest architectural achievement, the octagonal Selimiye Camii

Rüstem Paşa Camii: The interior is almost entirely covered with İznik tiles.

in Edirne. In this case the dome is supported on four freestanding piers and four buttresses projecting from the walls. Since all the surfaces of the walls and piers are covered with tiles, they merge together as part of an all-encompassing whole. However, in other ways, the decoration actually emphasises the structure, such as the polychrome voussoirs of the arches and the tiled roundels of calligraphy in the pendentives. The roundels bear the names of God, Muhammad, and the first four caliphs, as well as Hasan and Husein. They are repeated in another eight roundels in the spandrels over the arches of the outer arcade of the porch. These are easy

to miss, but they can even be seen from the street below. One of them reads: "Muhammad the Prophet of God, Peace be upon Him."

Rüstem Paşa Camii was built at the peak of quality in the İznik workshops. Using the underglaze technique (see page 89), the craftsmen executed bold, mostly floral designs that stand out clearly against a white background. While earlier in the sixteenth century flowers and arabesques were subtly intertwined in continuous, somewhat abstract patterns, here the individual flowers can be identified. The designs often strike a balance between botanically accurate representation and fantasy. The tulips, with their red petals com-

Rüstem Paşa Camii: The porch. Located under a low roof, the porch is very similar to that of Mihrimah Sultan Camii in Üsküdar, but its wall is lined with sumptuous İznik tiles. Two niches mirror the *mihrab* inside. This porch is used as a place of prayer by many people who work in the market below.

Overleaf
Detail of an İznik tile.

ing together at a point, contrast strikingly with the dominant blues. These prefigure the eighteenth-century obsession with tulips that gave the period its name as the tulip age. The formula for the brilliant red glaze, used here for the first time, has never been rediscovered. A strong characteristic of the tiles is the use of sinuous lines, running through the designs. It appears that different teams of craftsmen were responsible for the various walls without much coordination, and certain areas seem to involve a change of plan. In some places, particularly on the porch, there are careless repairs after an earthquake. However, the flowering tree

motifs in the *mihrab* and at the top of the *minber* are spectacular. It is worth taking time to look for details. For example, above the door in the wall on the left, as you face the *mihrab*, you will notice a panel of Kufic calligraphy. Its geometric form, reading both forwards and backwards, is very different from the flowing classical script elsewhere. It reads: "There is no God but God. Muhammad is the Prophet of God." The soffits under the galleries are elaborately carved and painted, and you should not miss the main doors of carved walnut with inlaid mother-of-pearl.

İznik Tiles

The İznik tiles in the late sixteenth-century Ottoman mosques represent a peak of artistic achievement. They speak for the aesthetic desires of the imperial court, as well as the technical skill and creative flair of artisans. While they embody diverse influences, they also possess their own unique character.

The manufacture of pottery in Anatolia goes back to ancient times, but not until the early fifteenth century did fine tilework appear in Ottoman architecture. This sudden flourishing of ceramic art in Bursa and Edirne appears to have been due to the arrival of craftsmen from the Timurid cities of Samarkand and Tabriz, where palaces were lined with beautiful tiles. Little is known of the artisans who worked on Yeşil Cami and Muradiye Camii in Bursa, but there is clear evidence of Central Asian and Chinese influences. Whether the Chinese motifs came from porcelain or silk is not known. Such exquisitely tiled interiors were not repeated until the next century, but they must have shown the potential of tiling in mosques and contributed to the launching of an indigenous Ottoman ceramic industry, based in İznik (Nicea).

The earliest pottery made in İznik, known as Miletus ware, was of red clay with a white slip underglaze and cobalt blue decoration, but in around 1480 production began of a completely different type of ceramic material, known as "fritware". This had first been made in Egypt 300 years earlier, but the composition was improved in İznik. It contained a high proportion of ground quartz mixed with white clay and a soda-lead frit. It was covered with a white slip with finer quartz particles. The result of the technical innovation at İznik was porcelain of remarkable whiteness, superior to any produced in Egypt, Syria or Persia. To this base the craftsmen added sumptuous designs, mainly in blue, but with the gradual addition of other colours. Like those who were responsible for the tiles in the Yeşil Cami in Bursa, they absorbed influences from Chinese porcelain and Italian majolica, but they interpreted these sources in their own fashion. Flower and leaf forms were combined with abstract shapes in sinuous arabesques. A new cross-fertilisation occurred when Selim I brought back artisans from Tabriz after conquering the city in 1514. The earliest products of the kilns at İznik were vessels, candlesticks and lamps, but by the early 1520s they were producing tiles.

Beyazit II was too ascetic in his taste to consider using decorative tiles in his imperial mosque, and his son Selim I was too preoccupied with expanding the empire to build any mosques. However, in the one built for him by his son Süleyman in 1522, beautiful tiled panels appear in the lunettes over the courtyard windows. The colours, of cobalt blue, turquoise and yellow, appear clear and luminous, and were kept separate by the "cuerda seca" (dry cord) technique. This technique is used in many early Ottoman mosques. Colours are prevented from flowing into each other by a line of special material, literally a dry cord, between them. The cord expands in the kiln and forms a barrier to glazes of different colours. Larger tiled panels flanking the entry to Selim I's tomb look almost like carpets hanging on the walls.

In Süleymaniye Camii, tiling is applied to the walls that surround the *mihrab*. Here a brilliant tomato red, known as "Armenian bole", was introduced for the first time. Although sparingly used, it seems to enhance the predominant blue so that the colours carry across the huge space. One of the most impressive uses of İznik tiles at Süleymaniye Camii was in panels with white calligraphy on a deep blue background. This same pattern is found in many other mosques.

The most extravagant use of İznik tiles can be seen in Rüstem Paşa Camii (page 84), where the red is more pervasive and the patterns are livelier. Here all the walls and structural piers are covered with tiles, making the interior a patternbook of tile designs. Some panels, such as one on the outside wall to the left of the main entrance, are far more pictorial than in the past, representing flowering trees and recognisable flowers, most notably the tulip. In Sokollu Mehmet Paşa Camii (page 98) the İznik tiles surpass all others. The architect Sinan restricted the tiling to the *qibla* wall around the *mihrab*. The integration of decorative design and calligraphy reaches a peak here.

By the time these three mosques were being decorated with tiles, the İznik potteries had changed to the underglaze technique, which gave the tiles a brilliant luminosity. They were first painted and then dipped into a liquid glaze before being fired.

Fine İznik tiles were still available when Sultan Ahmet Camii (Blue Mosque) was built in 1609, though the colours were beginning to lose their brilliance. After this time the potteries declined, and the tiles used on later mosques are inferior.

above and opposite left
Mihrimah Sultan
Camii, Edirnekapı:
The tall tympanum
walls, penetrated by
many windows under
the massive arches,
admit more light
than the half domes
of other mosques.
(See also the interior
view of the dome on
page 65.)

The mosque built in Üsküdar by Süleyman's daughter Mihrimah was complete in 1548. Fourteen years later, while overseeing the building of Rüstem Paşa Camii, she showed her exalted status by building a large, unique mosque inside the Edirnekapı gate in the Theodosian walls. Mosques were often designed to serve a particular population, and those at the city gates were conceived as places of worship for travellers arriving in the city. Built on the highest point in the old city and standing unusually tall, Mihrimah's new mosque was visible to travellers on the road from Edirne and to armies returning from campaigns in Europe. Like the towers and spires of medieval pilgrimage churches in Europe, like St Sernin in Toulouse, the high dome and minaret offered courage to tired wayfarers as they caught sight of it in the distance.

Because the interior of the Iskele mosque in Üsküdar is rather dark, it has been suggested that Mihrimah impressed on Sinan her desire for a space flooded with light. If so, she can hardly have been disappointed with this unique design. The architect reverted from the hexagonal and octagonal plans, used in his last four mosques, to a square plan. Eliminating half domes altogether, he simply carried the high dome on four huge arches closed by glowing window walls. With those around the dome, there are 104 windows. Except for low aisles, there are no subsidiary spaces to add structural support. To resist the outward thrust of the 20-metre wide dome he simply buttressed the corners with octagonal towers, capped with weight towers. Visually strong, these also give confidence in the strength of the structure.

The mosque is entered through a large garden courtyard, with an attractive fountain. The original *medrese*, which opens off the court is still in use as a religious school. A row of column bases, parallel to the front of the seven-bay porch, suggests that this mosque was originally provided with an outer porch, like those at Mihrimah Sultan's mosques in Üsküdar and at Rüstem Paşa Camii in Eminönü.

right
Mihrimah Sultan Camii, Edirnekapı: Exterior from the Theodosian walls. The octagonal corner towers help to withstand the thrust of the huge arches supporting the dome. The small domes in the foreground cover the *medrese*.

Molla Çelebi Camii:
View into the dome and
surrounding conches.

This small mosque, in a park on the shore of the Bosphorus, was built by Süleyman's chief justice Molla Mehmet Efendi. (The term *molla* refers to a senior member of the *Ulema*, the scholars of Muslim law.)

The mosque's court was removed when the road in front of it was widened, but an elegant five-bay porch remains. Behind this stands a dome surrounded by five half domes. This represents another ingenious and architecturally brilliant experiment by Sinan with a hexagonal plan. The architect placed two half domes on either side of the main dome, as he had done before in the Kara Ahmet Paşa Camii. But this time Sinan placed the *mihrab* in a rectangular extension of the prayer hall and added a fifth half dome over it. To create a corresponding effect on the opposite side, he framed the entrance portal with two free-standing columns. These support the northern arch. The result is that the six arches open out into generous curved recesses on all sides. The architect has created an interesting interplay between the rectangle of the outer walls and the billowing curves of the half domes.

Edirne 1568–75

Selimiye Camii,
Edirne: Arcades of
the court.

Selim II, who succeeded his father Süleyman in 1566, had not been first in line to the throne; his older and more popular half-brother Mustafa was the heir apparent. But, as the eldest son of Süleyman's beloved wife Hürrem, Selim had an advantage. Determined to ensure his succession, Hürrem fabricated a story in 1553 that Mustafa was plotting to usurp the throne, and persuaded Süleyman to have him strangled. When Süleyman died on a campaign in Hungary, his grand vizier Sokollu Mehmet made sure that Selim took his place, although he was far away in Kütahya. Fearing a hiatus, Sokollu brought Süleyman's body back to Istanbul in a litter, pretending that he was only sick. The plan succeeded and, despite his unpopularity, Selim ascended the throne. Süleyman's last remaining son, Selim did not fol-low in his father's footsteps as a great warrior and lawgiver. He has been accused of excessive devotion to the pleasures of the harem and to drink. He left the affairs of state to the very capable Sokollu, and the running of the palace to Nurbânu, his favourite *kadın* (concubine). Considering his reputation, it might be surprising that he became the patron of the greatest of all Ottoman mosques. But he was blessed with an architect at the peak of his creative powers. Sinan responded not to the qualities of the sultan, but to the opportunity for greatness. With the Şehzade, Süleymaniye and Rüstem Paşa mosques, Mimar Sinan had experimented with a variety of structural and spatial systems. He modestly characterised these as works of his apprenticeship. Now he was ready to create his masterpiece.

According to legend, Muhammad appeared to Selim in a dream and commanded him to build his imperial mosque at the former capital, Edirne, in Thrace. There in 1438 the innovative Üç Şerefeli Cami had supplanted the earlier Eski Cami as the Friday mosque. Now Selim eclipsed both of them with a monumental structure whose high dome and four minarets dominate the city. It looks down upon them from a low hill, and can be seen from miles around. Indeed it was an inspiring sight for Ottoman armies as they marched from Istanbul towards military goals in Central Europe. Sinan supported a dome 31.28 metres wide, almost exactly the same diameter as that of Aya Sofya, on eight remarkably slender piers. He made this structural feat possible by integrating every element into a perfectly coordinated whole. The exterior form is dynamic in the manner of a perfectly conceived Gothic cathedral. From the relatively plain lower walls, the structure rises in a series of steps to the drum of the dome and up to its crown. Buttresses, weight towers and small half domes clustering around it are all proportioned for stability and to make a harmonious whole. The many windows at each level demonstrate how Sinan pared down the structure to allow the

opposite
Selimiye Camii, Edirne:
The dome, as wide as
that of Aya Sofya, is
supported on eight
slender piers.

maximum amount of light to penetrate the entire interior.

An extremely significant aspect of Sinan's design is revealed by the entry to Selimiye Camii: that of his handling of scale. It is often said that, compared with the towering Gothic cathedrals of the medieval era, the architecture of the Italian Renaissance possessed a human scale. While this may be the case in fifteenth-century Florence, many Italian churches were monumental in scale. For example, the façade of Alberti's Sant' Andrea in Mantua

combines two overbearing architectural forms, the Roman temple front and the triumphal arch. Despite its harmonious proportions, it tends to dominate the space before it and dwarf the humans who stand before it. Sinan's approach was different. The mosque is indeed a vast domed structure, grand enough to honour the most exalted sultan (dominating the skyline of Edirne as it affirms the sultan's spiritual power), but as we approach and move through it, we experience a series of changing relationships with the building. First, we

Selimiye Camii, Edirne:
Plan and section. Six of
the eight piers are free-
standing; those
flanking the *mihrab* are
engaged to the wall.
Cornelius Gurlitt

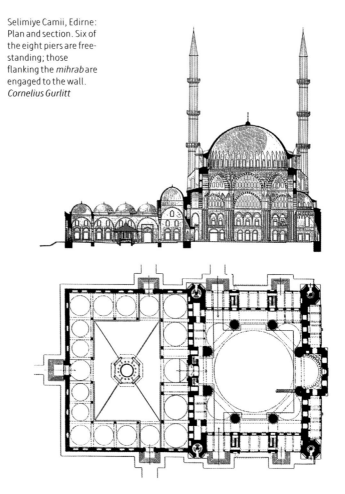

enter through a humble gateway in a low wall and pass through a peaceful garden, planted in a relatively informal manner. A second, simple gate, reached by a short flight of broad steps, leads into the arcaded court before the mosque. Although at this point it is close enough to be overpowering, the dome is framed in a manner that makes it approachable. Whereas the Gothic cathedral and the Renaissance façade rise cliff-like before us, the shady arcade before the entrance mediates with the mass of the dome. The weight towers stand forward, partially obscuring it and, at the same time, offering assurance that it will stand firm. Unlike Michelangelo, who felt obliged to conceal the buttresses around the dome of St Peter's with coupled Corinthian columns, Sinan expresses these structural elements as exactly what they are. If, rather than entering, we walk through the garden to the south side and look up at the outer walls, we are not confronted with a symbolic, applied façade like that of Alberti's Sant' Andrea, but the structural walls that support the dome and admit light from the sky.

As we enter the mosque, the scale changes. It is now that we are overwhelmed, as Sinan intended. The drama of entering is heightened by the human-scaled gateways and courtyard that precede the soaring prayer hall. The inside, built of the same honey-coloured sandstone, fulfils the promise of the outside view. No interior in western architecture before the twentieth century offers such a sense of unobstructed space. The structure is so well proportioned that Alberti's definition of beauty comes to mind: "The harmony and concord of all the parts achieved in such a manner that nothing could be added or taken away or altered except for the worse." However, the piers' simple and elegant design does not recall the work of Italian Renaissance architects. Their insistence on the application of classical orders with projecting columns and cornices produced less serene surfaces. The facets of the twelve-sided piers that support the dome have vertical lines incised in them. This device emphasises verticality and catches the light in a lively way, similarly to the fluting of a classical col-

umn. But these lines are interrupted by a horizontal moulding at the level where the lower arches spring, thus emphasising a line running all the way round the interior, and balancing the height with the width.

The piers terminate with understated capitals that gently make the transition to the pendentives. The pendentives in turn are enriched with a *muqarnas* pattern. Rather than creating a boldly patterned surface in the manner of the early Bursa mosques, Sinan has created no more than a ripple on the surface. The dominance of structure over applied ornament seems comparable to designs by some of the precursors of modern architecture at the end of the nineteenth century, for example Louis Sullivan in his Chicago Auditorium (1887–89). This is not that surprising, because Sinan was as much an engineer as an architect. Modernists appreciated the clean lines and functional expression of engineers, criticising architects for imitating historic styles and their obsession with decoration.

An unusual feature of Selimiye Camii is the *müezzin's* gallery in the

centre of the prayer hall, under which is a small fountain. This seems to be a reference to the traditional interior fountains of the Bursa mosques, such as the one in the Yeşil Cami. However, the main fountain for ablutions is in the courtyard.

There are many interior details to look at. You should not miss the exceptionally tall *minber*, delicately carved of Marmara marble, and the many inscriptions. The tiled walls and calligraphy on either side of the *mihrab* are superb. An excellent view of the interior can be enjoyed from the gallery over the entrance.

As you leave the mosque, pass through the market building on the west side, reached by a staircase from the garden court on that side. Sunk below the level of the mosque, it bolsters one side of the level platform on which the mosque stands.

Like the commercial property under Rüstem Paşa Camii in Istanbul (see page 85), it provides income for the religious foundation. The market was begun by Sinan, and finished after his death.

You may be surprised to find no tomb for Selim here. He chose, perhaps out of reverence for the great Byzantine structure, to be buried at Aya Sofya. With its excellent İznik tilework on the porch his tomb is well worth seeing, but the interior is closed.

opposite left
Selimiye Camii, Edirne: Distant view. The buttresses and weight towers surrounding the dome dramatise the structure.

opposite right
Selimiye Camii: The portal leading into the inner court is framed by trees. Visitors can walk in the peaceful garden before entering the mosque.

below
Selimiye Camii: Entrance to the inner court. The arcades mediate between the visitor and the vast mosque. When seen from here, the dome does not seem overbearing.

opposite
Sokollu Mehmet Paşa
Camii, Kadırga: The
İznik tiles on the Qibla
wall and pendentives
are among the finest.
Reha Günay

İsmihan Sultan, the eldest daughter
of Selim II and his consort Nurbânu,
commissioned this mosque jointly
with her husband Sokollu Mehmet
Paşa, Süleyman's last grand vizier.
As a young man Sokollu, the son of
a Bosnian priest, had been selected
by the *devşirme* to serve in the royal
household. He gained favour by
rescuing Haseki Hürrem from drown-
ing when her boat capsized, and
quickly rose from chief gatekeeper
to Grand Admiral and finally to
Grand Vizier of the Empire. When
Süleyman died during the siege of
Sziget in Hungary, Sokollu concealed
his death and brought his body back
to Istanbul, ensuring the accession
of Selim II and securing his own
place as Grand Vizier. His marriage
to Selim's daughter, İsmihan Sultan,
strengthened his position. Sokollu
effectively ran the empire for another thirteen years, and did his best
to sustain a moderating influence
on Selim. He even survived the
humiliating defeat, in 1571, of
the Ottoman navy at the Battle of

Lepanto. The fleet of a triple alliance
of Spain, Venice and the Papacy,
commanded by Don John of Austria,
routed the Ottomans with a loss of
280 ships and 30,000 lives. After this
defeat, the Ottoman fleet never
again dominated the seas.

Sinan skilfully fitted the mosque
onto the steep slope southwest
of the Hippodrome by raising the
buildings on the north side of the
court. A steep flight of steps, leading
up to the street below on the main
axis, gives a framed view of the
beautiful fountain. The lightness
and elegance of Sokollu's mosque,
built a year after the Ottoman defeat
at Lepanto, rises above the gravity
of the times. This was the last of
Sinan's designs to have a dome supported on six arches, and the most
successful. Having played a series
of variations on this structural system, using either four or six piers to
help support the dome, he eliminated the piers altogether and carried
the dome on buttresses attached to
the walls. The effect is serene and

spacious. If Sokollu was trying to
outdo Rüstem Paşa, his approach
was within a spirit of moderation.
The walls and piers are of plain, pale,
honey-coloured stone, but in contrast, the *qibla* wall under the south
arch is entirely covered, except for
the stone *mihrab*, with fine İznik
tiles. The roundels flanking the top
of the *mihrab* and those in the pendentives, with white inscriptions on
blue backgrounds, show the combination of abstract decoration and
calligraphy at its best. To either side
of the *qibla* wall, two arches open
out into the corners of the rectangular space. Since the dome is very
high, the arches seem tall and graceful. The view up into the dome is
made particularly attractive by the
predominantly blue tiles in the pendentives, which make a star shape
around its base. The six arches seem
to flow together in a continuous circular motion.

Four stones from the Ka'ba in
Mecca are built into the structure,
two above the *mihrab*, one over the
entrance door, and one on the *minber*. Another item of interest is the
pair of columns flanking the *mihrab*,
which are capable of rotating and
thus indicating settlement in the
structure.

Sokollu Mehmet Paşa
Camii: An arcade of
the courtyard.

Piyale Paşa Camii: The plan, with six small domes, is reminiscent of early Ottoman mosques in Bursa and Edirne.

When Piyale Paşa endowed this mosque, he was the powerful Grand Admiral of the Ottoman navy, as well as husband of Selim II's daughter Gevherhan. He gained the favour of Selim II for a series of relentless campaigns that added 69 Aegean islands to the Empire. His rise to power from humble origins as the son of a Croatian shoemaker shows how the *devşirme* system and education in the palace school rewarded individual merit. Today the mosque seems remote, but when it was built it stood at the head of a vast naval enclave. The Naval Arsenal on the shore of the Golden Horn below was at the height of its production, providing Piyale Paşa with ships for his voyages of conquest. The mosque was designed as a place of worship for seamen, and for elaborate ceremonies as thanks for naval victories.

There is some doubt that Sinan designed this mosque. It is unlike any other since the early fifteenth century. Instead of having the usual cluster of smaller domes and half domes around a large central dome, it embodies six equal domes in the manner of Ulucami in Bursa and Eski Cami in Edirne (see pages 26 and 36). But with Sinan Paşa Camii (page 83), Sinan had already shown his interest in revisiting historical types. Some scholars believe that this is another example of his constant experimentation. The domes, in two rows of three, are supported on two slender granite columns in the middle and on arches springing from piers in the surrounding walls. The result is quite unlike Ulucami with its bulky piers. The interior is lofty and spacious, flooded with light from the windows that fill the tympanum walls in the arches. A continuous band of calligraphy on İznik tiles runs all around the interior, level with the capitals of the columns, accentuating the effect of uninterrupted space. The *mihrab*, also decorated with fine tiles, stands out from the plain walls.

The exterior has been somewhat altered by the removal of porch roofs and some of the supporting columns after an earthquake, but the dominant features remain: the six domes and the tall arches. The arches rise rhythmically above the walls and create a strong impact. A particularly unusual feature is the minaret, placed centrally on the wall opposite the *mihrab*.

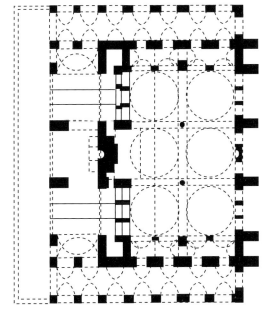

above
Zal Mahmut Paşa
Camii, Eyüp: The tall,
conventional arches
of the five-bay porch
contrast with the ogee
arches fronting the
medrese.

right
Zal Mahmut Paşa
Camii: Plan of the
mosque and two
medreses.

Zal Mahmut Paşa, the husband of
Süleyman's daughter Şahsultan,
became Selim II's fifth vizier in 1574.
He helped to clear the way for Selim's
succession to the throne in 1553 by
strangling his more popular brother
Mustafa. But he appears to have
played no significant role in running
the empire. The joint, posthumous
endowment of the mosque and
külliye, after the couple died on the
same day, offered Sinan another
opportunity for architectural experiment. Şahsultan's mother Nurbânu
supervised the construction. It is
built on sloping ground, which the
architect exploited by making a distinct change of level between the
mosque and *medrese* around a court
at the upper level, and an attractive
garden court with another *medrese*
below it. The alternating bands of red
brick and stone give the complex a
lively character, and there is variety
in the forms of the arcades around
the court. What distinguishes this

mosque from others is the way in
which the dome has been placed over
a rectangle. Four large arches define
a central square, above which the
dome is supported on pendentives,
but the interior space is extended to
the north, east and west by areas the
full width of the mosque, whose
many-windowed walls rise as high as
the drum of the dome. Galleries on
rather sturdy arcades fill the lower
stories of these extensions, reinforc-
ing the definition of the central
square and dramatising the light
flooding in from the upper windows.

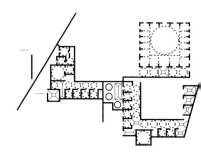

33 SOKOLLU MEHMET PAŞA CAMİİ (Itinerary G)
Azapkapı 1573–77/78

Sokollu Mehmet Paşa Camii, Azapkapı: Once again Sinan has varied the octagonal support system of the dome.

One of the most enduring of grand viziers, Sokollu Mehmet built this mosque (his second in Istanbul) while serving his third sultan, Murat III. He sited it at the north end of the Atatürk Bridge, only five years after his mosque in Kadırga. These are only two of the religious and charitable foundations endowed by him in various cities. Like the ubiquitous Rüstem Paşa, Sokollu made sure that his name was widely known. It is hardly surprising that he was enamoured of Selimiye Camii in Edirne, for he was running Selim II's empire while it was under construction. He seems to have asked Sinan to create a small version of it, but this mosque is no replica. From the bridge one can get a close view of the weight towers around the dome that stand above the eight piers below. They possess their own character, as do the interior piers. Like Rüstem Paşa Camii, the building is raised up over commercial, revenue-producing property. Indeed there are other similarities and subtle contrasts between the two designs. One aspect is that Rüstem Paşa's dome is surrounded by four half domes and four flat walls, while Sokollu's is encircled by eight half domes.

The assassination of Sokollu in 1589 is regarded as the event marking the end of the "classical age".

above
Atik Valide Sultan
Camii, Üsküdar:
The arcades on the
north side of the court
offer a human scale.

opposite
Atik Valide Sultan
Camii, Üsküdar.
The dome, framed
by an arch.

Nurbânu, the legal wife of Selim II, was of Venetian origin. During his reign she ruled the palace, and on his death, as the mother of his successor Murat III, she became the *Valide Sultan*. Wanting to maintain her control, she distracted her son from affairs of state by procuring the most beautiful women for him. He was a willing accomplice, fathering over a hundred children. Nurbânu's power increased when Sokollu Mehmet Paşa was assassinated in 1574. The end of his long and effective rule as grand vizier gave her the opportunity to take control, and ushered in a period when women were very powerful in the palace.

The large *külliye* endowed by Nurbânu on the high ground above Üsküdar shows her aspirations as a great patron. Including a *medrese*, elementary school, convent, hospital, hospice and caravanserai, it surpasses those of all the sultans except Mehmet II and Süleyman. As intended, it became the nucleus of a new urban neighbourhood. Although most of the *külliye* is inaccessible today, its outer walls can be seen to the southwest of the mosque.

The informal courtyard of Atik Valide Sultan Camii is approached through a small cemetery between two stone gateways. Entering to one side of the mosque, you will find yourself in a well-planted garden surrounded by graceful arcades. Sheltered by foliage, a circle of benches is a popular meeting place for neighborhood men. Two ancient plane trees, planted near the fountain when the mosque was built, still give pleasant shade. To the

right, you can see the dome and two minarets of the mosque behind the spreading roof of the double porch. The arcades of the court could be considered to be reminiscent, in their human scale, of Brunelleschi's architecture in fifteenth-century Florence. While the arcades of many imperial mosques are raised up in a formal manner above the paving of the court, these are level with the lawns and paths of the garden. It is worth descending to the lower court of the *medrese* on the north side to look up at the fountain and dome framed in an arch.

The mosque was originally built with a central dome on a hexagonal support system, with two half domes on either side and a fifth half dome over a protruding rectangle for the *mihrab*. The interior space was enlarged in the seventeenth century by the addition of two complete domes at either side. The result is a very wide space with the *mihrab* on the short axis. This effect is increased by the long row of columns supporting a gallery on the north side.

The plain white walls and piers enhance the effect of lightness achieved by the many windows in the dome, half domes and walls. They also accentuate the colours, predominantly blue, of the İznik tiles around the *mihrab*. These include exquisite panels representing vases with flowers, flanked by sinuous branches of foliage, along with panels of calligraphy above the lower windows.

left
Atik Valide Sultan Camii,
Üsküdar: İznik tiling.

opposite
Interior view.

opposite
Kılıç Ali Paşa Camii:
Interior. The longitudinal axis of the dome
and half domes is
further emphasised
by the galleries that
define the edges of the
central space, in the
manner of Aya Sofya.

below
Kılıç Ali Paşa Camii:
Dome and minaret.

The life of Kılıç Ali Paşa was so adventurous that it seems like fiction. Born in Italy, the son of a Calabrian fisherman, he intended to become a priest, but his plan was cut short when he was captured by Ottoman corsairs and spent many years as a galley slave. After converting to Islam, he was freed and became an officer in the Ottoman navy. For his outstanding leadership in several campaigns, he rose to power and prestige as Governor-General of Islands. After his distinguished performance in the otherwise disastrous Battle of Lepanto (1571) Selim II gave him the title Kiliç, meaning "sword", and appointed him Grand Admiral of the Ottoman fleet. The sultan's faith in him was justified when he recaptured Tunis, and returned from raids on the Italian coast with thousands of slaves and prodigious booty. He contributed to the rebuilding of the Ottoman fleet and played an important role in overseeing construction at Topkapı Palace and other sites. He was known for his genial disposition and generosity. Vigorous to the last, it is recorded that he died at the age of 87. He chose a site near the Bosphorus so that it would provide a congregational mosque for seamen when they were in harbour.

It is likely that the decision to model it on Aya Sofya may have been urged by the admiral. But it is clear that Sinan was still fascinated by the Byzantine church. For over 40 years, with brilliant results, he had pursued experiments in space, light and structure, constantly manipulating architectural elements to create buildings of individual character. With its central dome and two half domes, and an emphasis on the longitudinal axis, Kılıç Ali Paşa Camii follows Aya Sofya more closely than any other that Sinan designed. However it is not simply a shrunken version of the original; he has given it his own stamp. As he reduced the size, it was necessary for him to simplify it. For example, the exedrae of Aya Sofya, defined by curved screens of columns and arches opening to aisles and galleries beyond, have become large niches with windows in solid walls. As in his other mosques, the space is more finite and less mysterious than most Byzantine interiors. While at Aya Sofya the massive square piers and narrow arcades create a barrier between nave and aisles, Sinan has used round piers and broad arches to open up the space. The aspect that distinguishes this interior from any others is that here the galleries come right up to the edge of the central space. Sinan has reversed his tendency to push them back against the outer walls.

The exterior form combines the typical high dome and minaret with their vertical expression and one of Sinan's contributions to Ottoman architecture: the low, sheltering, double porch. However, while the porch in both Mihrimah Sultan Camii in Üsküdar and Rüstem Paşa Camii stands on a raised platform, here the prayer hall is at ground level. The porch roof sweeps down close to the approaching worshippers to create a human scale.

Over the central entry portal from the porch is a beautiful calligraphic inscription in gold leaf from the Qur'an: "He is Allah, the Creator, the Shaper out of Naught, the Fashioner. His are the most beautiful names. All that is in the heavens and earth glorifieth him and He is the Mighty, the Wise."

One of Sinan's last mosques, and almost his smallest, this building's inventive plan and picturesque position on the Bosphorus give it a special appeal. Şemsi Ahmet Paşa came from an ancient, noble family and became grand vizier without having to go through the *devşirme* system. But he appears to have been a subversive character. He plotted against Sokollu Mehmet Paşa before his assassination, and may well have played a part in it. Surviving a short while as grand vizier, he completed his mosque before being dismissed. Seen from the water the twin domes of the mosque and the *medrese*, one higher than the other, combine in a lively composition, with the tall minaret and the long wall enclosing the court. The L-shaped *medrese* is at right angles with the waterfront, while the mosque, oriented towards Mecca, is placed obliquely. Thus a triangular court is formed between the two buildings. Echoing the *medrese* shape, the porch of the mosque runs around two sides of the mosque and creates an intriguing dialogue with the *medrese* arcades. Now a public library, the glazing in the arches of the *medrese* weakens the interplay of the two forms. Entering by a gate from the east, you will pass through a small triangle between the two arcades, and enter the larger triangular space opening up to the water. A sense of enclosure is created by the stone wall between the Bosphorus and the court, although it is pierced by fifteen rectangular openings that frame sections of the view across the water. The tomb, unlike most others, is right up against the mosque and open to it from the inside.

below
Şemsi Ahmet Paşa Camii: Night view of the exterior.

below right
Şemsi Ahmet Paşa Camii: Plan.

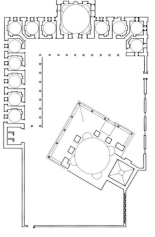

The *nişancı* was the chancellor of the Imperial council, a position held by Mehmet Paşa three times. A poet and calligrapher, it was his duty to write the sultan's monogram on documents. Sinan was still chief architect when his mosque was built (he died in the year of its completion), but his principal assistant Davut Ağa designed it. He took the octagonal scheme, on which Sinan had played several variations, and produced a new interpretation of it. Around the central dome, and supported on eight smooth, white columns engaged to the walls, rectangular recesses alternate with conches. The four rectangles extending the space at ground level may imply the form of a cross, which does not belong in Islamic architecture, but around the base of the dome there is a continuity of form. The half domes covering the rectangles (each with four windows), and those over the conches (with three windows), billow out from equal arches and create an undulating band of light. In the porch is some fine calligraphy, carved in stone and then gilded.

The interior form is clearly reflected on the exterior, where eight tall, slim weight towers alternate with lower and broader half domes. The attractive court is one of only two that were attached to mosques built by grand viziers.

Nişancı Mehmet Paşa Camii: Eight weight towers and eight small domes surround the main dome.

LATE CLASSICAL MOSQUES

After the death of Mimar Sinan in 1588, his pupil and chief assistant Davut Ağa was appointed chief architect. He had proved his ability with Nişancı Mehmet Paşa Camii and a few other projects, but his short tenure was not a time when large imperial mosques were endowed. He designed the fine tomb of Murat III beside Aya Sofya and made the original design for Yeni Valide Camii in Eminönü.

Executed for holding heretical beliefs, Davut Ağa was succeeded in 1599 by Dalgıç Ahmet Ağa, a good engineer, but undistinguished as architect. In 1606 Mehmet Ağa, who gained fame with the design of the Sultan Ahmet Camii (Blue Mosque), took over. Born a Christian in about 1540, Mehmet had probably begun his career in the Janissaries. He gained the attention of the young Ahmet I when he created a throne for him of walnut, mother-of-pearl and tortoise shell.

The architecture of this period – from the late sixteenth century to the early eighteenth century – was founded on the achievement of Sinan. It remained classical in character, but lacked the clarity of concept and the vigorous experimentation of the sixteenth century.

38 YENİ VALİDE CAMİİ (Itinerary C)
(New Mosque, or Yenicami)
Eminönü 1597–1603; 1660–63

above
Yeni Valide Camii, Eminönü: The spacious interior is based on the same structural scheme as the Şehzade Camii

left
Yeni Valide Camii, Eminönü: A complex cluster of half domes leads up to the main dome. On the hill, the Süleymaniye Camii can be seen.

The ferry landing at Eminönü to the east of the Galata Bridge is dominated by the cluster of large and small domes of Yeni Valide Camii. Although it looks stable today, it suffered an unfavourable beginning as well as a complex genesis under two *valide sultans*.

The mosque was begun by Safiye Sultan, the Venetian-born favourite of Murat III and mother of Mehmet III. To ensure the succession of her son, when Murat died in 1595 she had nineteen of his brothers strangled. She ruled the palace for seven years, and then she too was strangled, by a rival in the harem. Before her death she initiated the ambitious venture of building a huge mosque on marshy ground near the commercial hub of the city. In order to make

space for it, a community of Jews belonging to an unorthodox sect known as the Karai, were banished from the area. Davut Ağa designed Yeni Valide Camii with a plan based on Şehzade Camii, but did not survive to oversee its construction. He was perhaps fortunate, because the waterlogged site was unsuitable for the foundations of a vast structure. The problem was ingeniously solved by the next architect, Dalgıç Ahmet Ağa, who built a series of piers with bridges between them. He earned the name Dalgıç, meaning "diver", as an accolade for his underwater foundation work.

Mehmet III died a year after his mother, and Ahmet I who succeeded him in 1603 stopped the work. The Karai, whose compensation for the loss of their homes and synagogue had been embezzled, returned to squat in the structure that had not yet risen far above ground level. In 1660, after a fire broke out in the unfinished mosque, Turhan Hadice, the mother of Mehmet IV, saw the blackened ruin of Yeni Valide Camii and seized the opportunity of completing it as her *valide sultan külliye*.

Although 60 years had elapsed, the new architect, Mustafa Ağa, closely followed Davut Ağa's original plan. The completed mosque reveals that while Davut was grounded in the architecture of the classical era, he wanted to give the mosque its own character. The four half domes and myriad small domes and weight towers gathered around the main dome create a restless form. On the asymmetrical façades three tall arches announce the main entrances, juxtaposed with long arcades in two tiers. These elements enliven the walls by casting deep shadows. The

Below left
Yeni Valide Camii, Eminönü: Night view.

Below right
Yeni Valide Camii, Eminönü: A worshipper reading the Qur'an.

minarets, with three balconies on stalactite corbels, stand boldly at the junctions between the court and the body of the mosque. Now closed, the principal entrance to the court is approached by a grand flight of steps and surmounted by an inscription: "May health be yours. If you are worthy, enter for all eternity." The square courtyard contains an attractive octagonal fountain that is purely symbolic; ablutions take place, as in Süleymaniye Camii, along the outer walls of the mosque.

The interior, with its four half domes opening out from the central space, is arranged in a similar way to Şehzade Camii, but its proportions are a little different. The dome is two metres narrower and one metre higher, the piers are slightly more slender, but the changes that make the most difference are the galleries encroaching on both sides of the space and the smaller windows. These factors, as well as the pollution of Eminönü, rob this mosque of the brightness of the Şehzade.

Today all of the *külliye* buildings have disappeared, except the large market now known as the Egyptian Market or the Spice Market.

opposite above
Sultan Ahmet Camii:
By building six
minarets, this Sultan
outdid all others.

opposite below
Sultan Ahmet Camii:
Light penetrates
through rings of
windows below the
dome and half domes.

The most visited of all the mosques of Istanbul is Sultan Ahmet Camii – more popularly known as the Blue Mosque – but the circumstances of its founding were hardly propitious. While Süleyman the Magnificent endowed his mosque at the peak of a glorious reign, his great, great grandson Ahmet I built his at a time of weakness. Ahmet succeeded the throne in 1603 at the age of thirteen. Early on in his reign he showed signs of strength and courage, but was later accused of allowing his harem and his chief eunuch too much influence. His habit of choosing incompetent viziers and rapidly dismissing them also caused instability. Only three years into his reign, with no prospect of military success in Hungary, Ahmet signed the treaty of Zsitvatorog, which released the emperors of the Holy Roman Empire, as kings of Hungary, from the obligation to pay tribute to the sultan.

By way of an offering to please God, Ahmet decided to build a great mosque. Previous sultans had begun such projects when their coffers were bursting with the spoils of war, but Ahmet had no such reserves. His plan to build on such a grand scale and to raise six minarets aroused great disapproval because only in Mecca had so many minarets been built. Adding to the cost of construction, his choice of site required the demolition of valuable property, including the palace built by Sokollu Mehmet Paşa. Despite all the objections, however, the mosque was begun without much delay. It was completed a few months before Ahmet died of typhus.

Most imperial mosques were in sparsely populated areas of Istanbul to encourage development of urban districts, but against considerable opposition Ahmet made the bold decision to place his in the heart of the old city, close to Aya Sofya. Ironically, his mosque was greatly favoured by future sultans for Friday prayers. Its position made it ideal for special ceremonies, as it was conveniently close to Topkapı Palace and the Hippodrome. Ahmet's arrogant insistence on getting his own way saved him from obscurity and made his name one of the best known in Istanbul.

If you stand in the formally landscaped space between Aya Sofya and the Sultan Ahmet Camii, you will see the dynamic relationship between the two structures, built almost 1100 years apart. They are like two members of a family, yet distinct in their character.

The architect was Mehmet Ağa, who based his design on Sinan's Şehzade Camii as Davut had done in Yeni Valide Camii. Once again, four equal half domes radiate from a main dome. These elements, and many other smaller ones around them, rise progressively in a great pyramid to the finial. Although the Sultan Ahmet Camii is not as high as Süleymaniye Camii, the effect on the skyline, further enhanced by the six minarets, is magnificent, whether seen from the Sea of Marmara or the urban spaces around it. The walls are plain, the portals are not extravagant, and there is no elaboration in the courtyard arches. The mosque is seen as a whole without the distraction of details.

Inside the mosque the diminished height is evident, and painted decoration seems to dominate over the structure and space. Despite their ribbed surfaces, the "elephant's foot" columns seem more massive than those of Sinan's mosques. The

space, for all its grandeur, does not
soar in the manner of the Şehzade
and the Süleymaniye, as its immense width competes with the
height.

The entire production of the İznik
potteries was required to satisfy
Ahmet's obsessive desire for tiles.
While 20,000 were lavished on his
mosque, the potteries were forbidden to sell to anyone but the sultan.
Although the colours had lost their
brilliance by the time of this project,
the tiles contribute to the richness of
the interior. Their predominantly blue
colour, echoed in the painted decorations, gave the mosque its name.
Unfortunately the best panels of
tiling are in the galleries, where the
public cannot see them at close hand.

Sultan Ahmet Camii,
with the Sea of
Marmara in the
background.

above
Çinili Cami: İznik tiles in the *mihrab*.

above right
Çinili Cami: The interior is tiled up to the springing of the dome. Note the calligraphy in the lunettes.

Ahmet I died young, in 1617, and his favourite wife, the Greek-born Kösem, was dispatched to the old palace. Two weak sultans followed in quick succession, but after the assassination of Osman II by the Janissaries in 1622, Kösem returned in triumph as *valide sultan* when her son came to the throne as Murat IV. She continued to wield enormous power throughout the reigns of Murat and her son Ibrahim. Built in the year of Ibrahim's succession by an unknown architect, the small Çinili Cami scarcely proclaims her status as one of the most influential women in Ottoman history.

The mosque and *medrese* stand on a small sloping site northeast of Atik Valide Sultan Camii in Üsküdar.

The architect took advantage of the slope to place the mosque in the upper corner, where it overlooks the irregularly shaped courtyard, and increased its dominance by raising it on a high platform. The attractive, informal court, with its large roofed fountain, is planted with trees and flowers. In the simple square-domed prayer hall, pride of place is given to the İznik tiles that cover the walls and the *mihrab*, up to the springing of the pendentives. Bold calligraphy in the lunettes over the openings contrasts with delicate plant and flower designs elsewhere. Although the tiles lack the brilliant reds and greens made in the heyday of the İznik potteries, they give the mosque a delightful character.

BAROQUE PERIOD MOSQUES

The Baroque style originated in Rome during the seventeenth century, partly in reaction to the Protestant Reformation. Its flamboyant forms were intended to celebrate a triumphant Catholic church. It was also a passionate alternative to the cool, intellectual nature of High Renaissance Classicism. The essence of the Italian Baroque lay in the complexity of plan, the dramatic manipulation of space and light, and the integration of architecture, painting and sculpture. Curvilinear forms were prevalent.

By the eighteenth century, the Baroque in Europe had given way to neo-Classicism and a return to more conventional designs. However, it was at this time that the Ottomans began to develop a greater interest in European civilisation. Ahmet III (1703–30) asked the ambassador he sent to Paris to learn about French customs and styles. European clothing became fashionable, but many years were to pass before religious architecture was influenced. Surprisingly the Baroque style, by now outdated in Europe, appeared first, but it made little impact on the plans of mosques. At the insistence of the *Ulema*, the domed rectangle prevailed over more original plans. Since figurative painting and sculpture was proscribed by Islamic law, the fusion of art and architecture did not occur. As a result, Baroque characteristics tended to be superficial and decorative. In mosques such as the Nuruosmaniye and the Nusretiye, a new energy appeared in the expression of structural forces; but in others, such as Yeni Valide Camii at Üsküdar, the Fatih and the Eyüp Sultan mosques, the design was essentially Classical.

Nuruosmaniye Camii: View of the lavish Baroque interior.

left
Yeni Valide Camii,
Üsküdar: The octagonal
dome rises out of a
square base.

above
Yeni Valide Camii: The
mihrab and *minber* are
little more elaborate
than those of the
classical era.

opposite
Yeni Valide Camii: The
interior is structured
like that of Rüstem
Paşa, but lower.

The reign of Ahmet III (1703–30) ushered in a period of diplomacy and peace with Europe. Ahmet was a passionate builder and a patron of the arts and literature, and delighted in sponsoring festivities. His chief architectural creations were gardens and pleasure palaces, while the most famous of his entertainments was the annual Tulip Fête in April, which showed the Ottoman passion for tulips at its peak. It is not therefore surprising that his time is known as the "Lale Devri", the Reign of the Tulip. These interests seem to have distracted him from building an imperial mosque, but he did endow Üsküdar's Yeni Valide Camii in honour of his mother, Gülnûş Emetullah. Perhaps he would have built an innovative mosque in his own name if he had not been deposed in the Patrona Halil uprising.

Although the Üsküdar mosque is included here under the Baroque heading (because it contains some Baroque features), it really belongs to the Late Classical period. Most unusual is the *türbe* standing at the front of the complex. Its elaborately carved openwork walls reveal that the interior of the tomb is a garden. The *sebil* (kiosk serving cups of water from a cistern) and the fountain in the court also show an elaboration hinting at the Baroque.

The mosque is an octagon within a square. It is structurally similar to Rüstem Paşa Camii, but lower. The decoration in the form of tiles and paint is somewhat overdone.

Nuruosmaniye Camii: The elements are articulated so as to stand out boldly and cast heavy shadows. See also interior view on page 121.

The dome of Nuruosmaniye Camii rises vigorously above the low skyline of the Bazaar quarter. With its four great arches on the exterior, visibly supporting the dome, it follows the precedent of Sinan's Mihrimah Sultan Camii at Edirnekapı (see page 90). While Sinan expressed a serene unity in his design, the various elements of Nuruosmaniye Camii are strongly articulated. Square corner piers are separated from dominant weight tow-ers by a broad cornice. Sharply mould-ed arches overhang the tympanum walls, casting deep shadows, and the lower edge of the dome oversails the buttresses around the drum.

Reflecting the obsession with light in the Baroque era, the archi-tect has increased the ratio of glass to stone. The huge windows in the tympana almost touch the arches, and the windows in the base of the dome are larger than usual. It is therefore not surprising, on enter-ing, to see two arcs of light coming together between the pendentives. Indeed, light is a theme of the mosque. When Osman III completed it after the death of his brother Mahmut I, who initiated the project, he named the mosque "Light of Osman" (Nuruosmaniye). Little is known about the designer, who was probably a Greek named Simeon, but he clearly had experience out-side the office of the imperial archi-tect. Baroque features, discouraged by the *Ulema* in the main body of the mosque, abound on details, notably the elaborate gateway and drinking fountain on the west side. But the most inventive feature is the horse-shoe-shaped court, whose arcades open through horseshoe arches. This is a dynamic space compared with the familiar rectangular courts.

43 LALELİ CAMİİ (Itinerary C)

(Tulip Mosque)

1759–63

Laleli Camii: The south wall shows a restrained use of the Baroque style.

Mustafa III's attractive mosque is raised up above a market to the west of Istanbul University. The market's commercial activity supported the *külliye* above, as with Rüstem Paşa Camii (page 84). The effect, however, is different. While Rüstem Paşa Camii is almost invisible from the narrow streets around it, Laleli Camii has a strong impact as it stands high above Ordu Caddesi. The mosque is elevated on a basement story above its broad paved terrace. This dramatic exploitation of height contributes more to the Baroque character than the decorative details. The architect, Mehmet Tahir Ağa, chose an octagonal support system for the dome, and made an innovative three-stage transition from the cubic lower walls to the drum of the dome. An octagonal story with arches and small half domes on alternate facets is inserted between them. As a counterbalance to the verticality, a long arcaded gallery runs the full width of the second story.

Height is also expressed inside the mosque, where eight unusually slender columns, with walls and conches close behind them, rise to support polychrome arches and the dome. Lavishly, perhaps excessively, ornamented with coloured marbles, the interior is lit by the many windows, which bring out the contrasting colours of the marble.

Beside the mosque, a grand flight of steps goes up to the entrance of the court. The rather mannered doorway, along with the change of material from stone to stripes of brick and stone, diminish the mosque's unity. Between the mosque and court, the minarets, whose shafts resemble Corinthian columns, stand on massive bases. Most of the subsidiary buildings have disappeared, but the tomb of Mustafa and his son Selim (assassinated by the Janissaries) survives. It is worth descending to the market in the undercroft where a huge octagonal room has a fountain at its centre.

opposite
Fatih Camii: Interior.

below
Fatih Camii: Buildings of the original *külliye*, in the foreground, survived the earthquake. The new mosque follows the structural scheme of the Şehzade Camii.

Following the destruction of the original mosque in a devastating earthquake in 1766, Mustafa III ordered the construction of a new Fatih Camii on the same foundations. Its design is based on the plan of Şehzade Camii (page 70) and Sultan Ahmet Camii (page 116), where a central dome is surrounded by four half domes. Although it was built in the Baroque period, the architect, who was probably Mehmet Tahir Ağa, reverted in many respects to the Classical style. (The original mosque is discussed on page 53.)

The tomb of Eyüp al Ensari from the inner court. Sultans were ritually girded with the sword of Osman on the platform with the ancient plane tree.

Eyüp al Ensari hosted the Prophet Muhammad as his guest when he first came to Medina and was one of the first in the city to convert to Islam. He became the Prophet's standard bearer, and was the last of his companions to survive. His final role was as one of the commanders of an Arab army that besieged Constantinople during the Umayyad era. They did not succeed in breaching the walls of the Byzantine city; in the late seventh century the aged Eyüp al Ensari died and was buried outside the walls, and the siege was lifted. When Mehmet II conquered the city in 1453 he miraculously rediscovered Eyüp's body and honoured him as a martyr by building a tomb and mosque for him.

The district of Eyüp became one of the most important pilgrimage places for Muslims after Mecca and Jerusalem. It was also at Eyüp that the sultans established their legitimacy when they succeeded to the Ottoman throne. As part of a dramatic ceremony, equivalent to the coronation of a European monarch, the new sultan would process from Topkapı palace to Eyüp by boat, to be received at Eyüp's tomb by the Chief Mufti and Sword Bearer. Standing by two ancient plane trees on a raised platform between the mosque and the tomb, such officials as the Grand Master of the Mevlevî Dervishes girded him with the sword of Osman. He then re-entered the city by the Edirne Gate and visited the tombs

Eyüp Sultan Camii:
The outer court
with the dome and
minarets.

of his ancestors at several imperial
mosques, before returning to the
palace. Thus he reaffirmed the continuity of his succession.

The original mosque and tomb
were destroyed after an earthquake,
but were rebuilt in the late eighteenth century by Selim III. As you
approach them, you pass through a
modern plaza with fountains before
entering an attractive outer court.
The irregular planning of this space,
with two Baroque gates as well as
an oblique view of the dome and
minarets, creates a dynamic quality.
It is often crowded with eager pilgrims. From there you proceed to
the quieter inner court. On one side
is the wall of Eyüp's tomb, covered
with İznik tiles. There is often a line

of pilgrims waiting to enter. You are welcome to join them as long as you are dressed appropriately. However, if the tomb is busy, it is advisable to visit the mosque first, because the exit from the tomb takes you back to the outer court. Next to the tomb you will see the platform where the sultans were girded with the sword of Osman. Beside a newly planted tree is one surviving ancient, hollow plane tree, within railings whose finials resemble the Mevlevî whirling dervishes's hats.

Although the mosque was built in the period when the Baroque style flourished, it is restrained in character. Its interior possesses an unusual quality. Avoiding decorative quirks, the architect concentrated on creating an appealing brightness. Many tall rectangular windows penetrate the high walls and illuminate the pale stone. Their light catches the gilded decoration on the *mihrab* and *minber* and the many surfaces of white marble. The dome, supported on an octagon within the rectangle, seems secondary to the luminous walls. As you go out through the generous porch, note the unusual capitals, based loosely on the Ionic order. The tomb is the typical octagon, but it is enclosed within a larger rectangular building, through which pilgrims pass with reverence. The tiles that cover it, inside and out, are not original, but they add colour and vitality.

Eyüp Sultan Camii: Interior. Many tall windows light the spacious interior.

Nusretiye Camii: The flamboyant corner buttresses and weight towers around the dome contribute to the Baroque character.

As this mosque was nearing completion, its patron Mahmut II named it the "mosque of divine victory". He was not celebrating the conquest of foreign lands, but the elimination of the Janissaries. This elite force had fought with many sultans to expand the borders of the Ottoman Empire, but they had resisted reform, revolted several times, and even deposed sultans. Mahmut was intent on creating a modern army, and when the Janissaries rose against him, his new rival force massacred them in their barracks.

Mahmut's architect was Krikor Balian, the first of a family of French-educated Armenians who would serve the sultans for the rest of the nineteenth century. One of the most exuberant Baroque mosques, seen from the Bosphorus it rises forcefully and many of its elements stress verticality. Like Nuruosmaniye Camii, its plan is a version of Mihrimah Sultan Camii in Edirnekapı, in which four corner piers support the arches carrying the dome (see page 90). Because there are no exedrae and half domes extending the interior space, the outer walls of both the mosques rise sheer. But the difference between the elegant restraint of Sinan and Balian's Baroque elaboration is very clear. The corner piers at Edirnekapı merge smoothly with the walls and are capped with simple weight towers. In contrast, those of Nusretiye Camii stand forward boldly, flare out at the top with cornices, and terminate with bulbous turrets in two stages. Continuing the vigorous upthrust, the closely spaced buttresses that surround the drum of the dome continue up as flamboyant pinnacles.

The view from the street is less unified. Balian fronted the mosque with royal apartments on either side of a high entrance arcade. Standing close by, one is almost unaware of the mosque; the appearance is more that of a small Italian palace. But of course the tall, slender minarets with two balconies proclaim its purpose. The palace façade of early Renaissance character is a strange companion to the bulbous bases of the minarets and the pavilions on the north side with undulating walls and decorative festoons. The interior is a single, large, square room. The abundant light falls on white marble accented with gold, and ornamented with some Baroque details.

above left
Nusretiye Camii: Distant view showing slender minarets.

above right
Nusretiye Camii: The interior form is simple; only the ornament is Baroque.

LATE NINETEENTH-CENTURY MOSQUES

The transitions in Ottoman architecture that took place under European influence were gradual. As we have seen, the Baroque style of the eighteenth century was only evident in the decorative treatment of such elements as window surrounds and corner towers. The fundamental form of Ottoman mosques changed little. But gradually architects in Istanbul began to introduce the classical language of architecture. For example, somewhat classical engaged columns appear in the Nusretiye Camli of 1820. By the mid-nineteenth century, Neoclassicism had become a dominant style. Façades of mosques were articulated with Roman columns and cornices, reminiscent of Italian palaces, their windows capped with little pediments. And yet Neoclassical designs were often enlivened with flourishes of a distinctly Baroque character. In the three mosques illustrated in this section, we will see no single style in the late nineteenth century, but a willingness to depart from Ottoman tradition.

above left
Dolmabahçe Camii:
View into the dome.
The curving windows
beneath the main arch-
es break with Ottoman
tradition.

above right
Dolmabahçe Camii:
The *mihrab* and
minber retain their
Ottoman form in the
Neoclassical space.

opposite
Dolmabahçe Camii:
The corner towers are
Baroque, while the
minarets, resembling
Corinthian columns,
are distinctly
Neoclassical.

In 1853 Sultan Abdülmecit (1839–61) moved out of the Topkapı Palace and into the grand Dolmabahçe Palace on the Bosphorus, designed for him by Karabet and Nikoğos Balian. They were the son and grandson respectively of Krikor Balian, who 20 years earlier had designed the flamboyant Nusretiye Camii.

This grandiose structure, with a marble façade almost 300 metres long on the waterfront, was built to show the world that the sultan could match European sovereigns in up-to-date architectural splendour. In fact, it masked the financial plight of the country. "Dolmabahçe" means filled-in garden. The palace was so named because Ahmet I had filled in the shore in the seventeenth century to extend a royal garden established by Selim I. In the year when Abdülmecit moved his court into the palace, he built the Dolmabahçe mosque for his mother Bezmialem Sultan.

Nikoğos Balian studied in Paris with Henri Labrouste, a progressive architect who experimented with the honest expression of structure and has been characterised as a romantic rationalist. Critics have not treated Balian's design very kindly. The semi-circular bands of windows under the great arches supporting the dome are considered too brash. But they show a desire to express structure in a modern way; the architect succeeds in breaking with the old Ottoman pattern of tympanum walls with many small windows. The corner towers, repeating the excessive palace decoration, are most elaborate. The minarets take the form of slender Corinthian columns in which the capitals, with acanthus leaves, support the balcony.

Mecidiye Camii, Ortaköy: The façades with their engaged columns are Neoclassical.

Abdülmecit began his own mosque only a year after the one he built for his mother. He chose an appealing site jutting out into the Bosphorus in the village of Ortaköy. The architects, Karabet and Nikoğos Balian, played a variation on the theme of the two previous mosques by members of their family. Like the Nusretiye and Dolmabahçe mosques, the dome is supported on four major arches stabilised by corner towers. Again the towers, rising from square shafts, are treated as decorative features. The main difference is that the tympanum walls beneath the arches resemble High Renaissance palace façades, with four columns each that stand forward to frame the windows. The low profile of the dome and its understated buttresses allow the walls to become the most important elements. But for the square plan and the interior flooded with light, Ottoman tradition has been eclipsed by European Classicism. Compared to Sinan's design for Mihrimah Sultan Camii at Edirnekapı, whose unadorned corner towers and bold arches express their structural purpose, this mosque displays architectural excess.

Hamidiye Camii:
The eclectic interior
combines Gothic,
Chinese and Islamic
elements.

Abdülhamit II (1876–1909) reigned as an absolute ruler, turning against the *Tanzimat* reforms of Abdülmecit, suspending the constitution, and dissolving parliament. Despite his power, he feared attack from the sea and chose not to live in Dolmabahçe Palace. Instead, he secluded himself at Yıldız where his father Abdülmecit and his uncle Abdülaziz had built pavilions in the park. The sultan turned Yıldız Palace into a well-guarded fortress; he built additional pavilions so that he could constantly sleep in different places, and constructed the mosque outside the gate to avoid going into the city for Friday prayers.

One would never guess the historical context in which this rather playful mosque was built. It is truly eclectic, in the spirit of the late nineteenth century, and combines elements from several styles in an Orientalist manner. The windows seem to belong to the eighteenth-century English Gothick of London's Strawberry Hill; a pair of columns framing the entrance to the space under the dome support brackets of distinctly Chinese character, and these are separated by an arch recalling Mughal India. The pale blue dome covered with gold stars floats etherially above the interior, with a sense of fantasy that evokes that of Regency England's Brighton Pavilion. Ironically this is almost the only place where the reclusive Abdülhamit was seen by his subjects. This mosque indicates a different side of the sultan's character – his interest in the arts. He opened art academies throughout the nation and did much to improve education. Skilled in woodwork, he even did some of the wood carving in his own mosque.

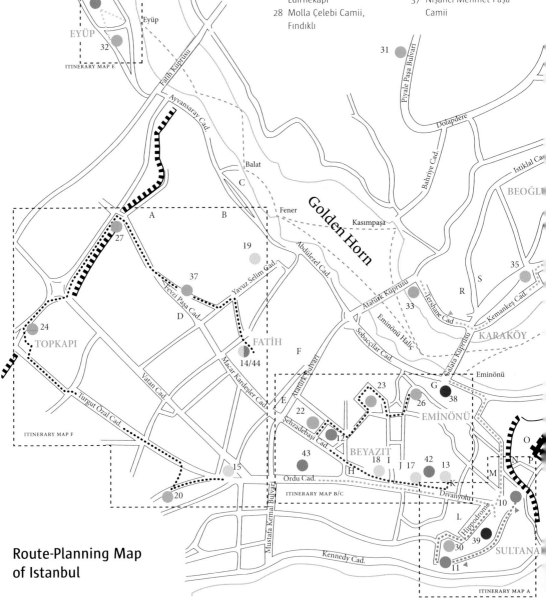

Route-Planning Map
of Istanbul

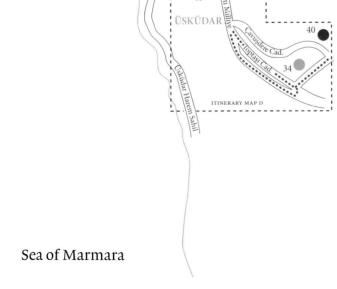

Late Classical Mosques

38 Yeni Valide Camii
   (Yenicami), Eminönü
39 Sultan Ahmet Camii
   (The Blue Mosque)
40 Çinili Cami (Tiled
   Mosque), Üsküdar

Baroque Period Mosques

41 Yeni Valide Camii, Üsküdar
42 Nuruosmaniye Camii
43 Laleli Camii
14/44 Fatih Camii
45 Eyüp Sultan Camii
46 Nusretiye Camii
   (Victory Mosque,
   or Tophane Mosque)

Late Nineteenth-Century Mosques

47 Dolmabahçe Camii
48 Mecidiye Camii, Ortaköy
49 Hamidiye Camii, Yıldız
   Palace

Key to Other Sites in Istanbul

The letters are located roughly in order as you go across the map (A to the left, Z to the right).

A St Savior in Chora
B Church of Pammacharistos
C St Stephens of the Bulgars
D Mosque of the Holy Mantle
E Valens Aqueduct
F Church of the Pantocrator
G Spice Bazaar
H Calligraphy Museum
I Book Bazaar
J Grand Bazaar
K Column of Constantine
L Museum of Turkish and
   Islamic Arts
M Basilica Cistern
N Imperial Mint
O Archaeological Museum
P Hagia Eirene
Q Topkapı Palace
R Galata Tower
S Mevlevi Monastery
T Military Museum
U Dolmabahçe Palace
V Naval Museum
W Çırağan Palace
X Yıldız Palace
Y Yıldız Park
Z Leander's Tower

Key to Itineraries (see pages 140–150), Walls and Ferry Lines

············ **Itinerary A**
The Byzantine Legacy
············ **Itinerary B**
The Evolution of the Ottoman Mosque
············ **Itinerary C**
Late Classical and Baroque Mosques
·········· **Itinerary D**
The Mosques of Üsküdar
············ **Itinerary E**
The Pilgrimage Site of Eyüp
•••••••••• **Itinerary F**
Fatih, Selim and Along the Landwalls
············ **Itinerary G**
Beyoğlu and the Bosphorus Shore

▪▪▪▪▪▪▪▪▪ Byzantine walls
– – – – – – Ferry lines

BEŞİKTAŞ

ORTAKÖY

Barbaros Bulvarı

Çırağan Cad.

Beşiktaş Cad.

Kadıgarlar Cad.

Dolmabahçe

Beşiktaş

Bosphorus

Üsküdar

Paşa Limanı

Sahil Yolu

Hakimiyeti Milliye

Çavuşdere Cad.

Toptaşı Cad.

Üsküdar Harem Sahil

ÜSKÜDAR

ITINERARY MAP D

Sea of Marmara

ITINERARIES with Local Maps

These walking itineraries are intended to lead you efficiently to a series of mosques. By following them you should avoid getting lost in a rabbit warren of streets and will save time and effort, but be prepared for narrow, steep and irregular streets. I have given clear walking instructions, but in some districts the street names are hard to find, or they may have been changed since publication. I have included some information on public transport, but you should check this yourself as routes and numbers may change. Improvements are being made: the tramway has been extended over Galata Bridge to Kabataş (between Karaköy and Beşiktaş), and it is also connected to Taksim Square by a funicular at Kabataş. Since taxis are plentiful and inexpensive, a few taxi rides on some of the longer stretches would make sense.

Turks are generally very honest, but you should beware of pickpockets in areas frequented by tourists.

As you go along the recommended routes, you will find page references for the detailed descriptions of the mosques. The maps have been simplified to make them readable, but the relationship of mosques to the surrounding streets and the distances between them are accurate. The scales of the maps vary according to the complexity of the street layout and the space available.

Itinerary A

The Byzantine Legacy
See map opposite

This itinerary includes Justinian's great church of Hagia Sophia (Aya Sofya) and the small octagonal church of SS. Sergius and Bacchus (Küçük Ayasofya), which lies nearby on the shore of the Sea of Marmara. Visits to these two masterpieces of Byzantine architecture will show the strength of the Byzantine legacy to the Ottomans. To help make the link between the two traditions, the walk finishes with a visit to the nearby Sokollu Mehmet Paşa Camii. The connection between the octagonal dome of SS. Sergius and Bacchus and the hexagonal one of Sokollu Mehmet Paşa Camii is striking. Since this mosque is open only at prayer times, you will need to plan your timing carefully. If you want a completely Byzantine day, you could go on to the church of St Savior in Chora. However, because of its location, it might make sense to combine it with Itinerary F.

Route for Itinerary A
Begin at Aya Sofya (mosque 10; page 41), which is conveniently close to the Sultanahmet stop on the tramway. After exiting, turn left on the Ayasofya Meydanı, the large paved area in front of you, and turn right at the end onto the cobbled Kabasakal Caddesi. Turn left at the end of this, and almost immediately go right down some steps into the Arasta Bazaar. Pass between two rows of carpet and antique shops. When you emerge, continue straight ahead into Küçük Ayasofya Caddesi (or, if you are looking for a restaurant, turn right into Tavukhane Sokak and try the one suggested at the end of this itinerary). Go downhill on Küçük Ayasofya Caddesi, past hotels and carpet shops, and you will soon see the dome and minaret ahead. At the foot of the hill, there is a crossroads with a small, planted island. On the right you will see some craftshops including the studio of a fine

calligrapher, Fuat Başar. The gate to Küçük Ayasofya (11; page 47) is on the left. The mosque has recently been restored. Make sure to go up a staircase to the gallery where the pristine Byzantine capitals can be seen against plaster walls without painted decoration. On the right is a charming courtyard with a café where you can have a drink or snack.

Leave Küçük Ayasofya by the same gate and turn left along a narrow cobbled street with chimneys on the left. Curve round to the right into Bardakçı Sokak. Go left at the T-junction ahead, but glance right at the ruined domed building with a small fountain in front of it. If you are looking for an inexpensive restaurant catering to local people you will find Çeşme Restaurant on the right, just before the ruin. They serve quickly from a selection of kebabs, salads and pide.

After going left at the T-junction, curve round to the right again on Kadırga Limanı Caddesi. You will see the minaret of Sokollu Mehmet Paşa Camii up the first turning on the right, but to enter it in the best way, wait until the second street on the right, and climb a flight of steps leading to the courtyard (30; page 98). After visiting this mosque, go out of the gate at the left-hand end of the porch (as you look at it from the court) and turn right up the hill. Keep straight on over a crossroads, and turn left at the top. After 50 yards you will find yourself at the southern end of the Hippodrome. Walk straight on and you will reach the tramway. Or, if you take the first right as you reach the Hippodrome, on Tavukhane Sokak you will come to Türkistan Aşevi, a restaurant in a traditional Ottoman house beautifully decorated with fine carpets and copperware, serving traditional Turkoman food.

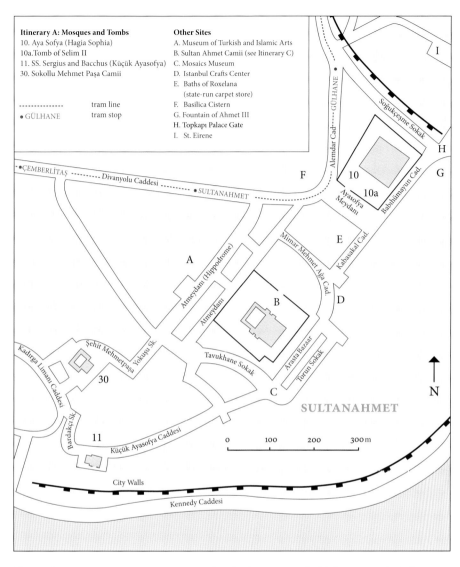

Itinerary A: Mosques and Tombs
10. Aya Sofya (Hagia Sophia)
10a. Tomb of Selim II
11. SS. Sergius and Bacchus (Küçük Ayasofya)
30. Sokollu Mehmet Paşa Camii

.... tram line
● GÜLHANE   tram stop

Other Sites
A. Museum of Turkish and Islamic Arts
B. Sultan Ahmet Camii (see Itinerary C)
C. Mosaics Museum
D. Istanbul Crafts Center
E. Baths of Roxelana
    (state-run carpet store)
F. Basilica Cistern
G. Fountain of Ahmet III
H. Topkapı Palace Gate
I. St. Eirene

Itinerary B

The Evolution of the Ottoman Mosque
See map on page 143

This itinerary is highly recommended as an introduction to the mosques of Istanbul. It would be best to walk it after seeing Aya Sofya. With visits to six mosques, it shows how Ottoman architects experimented with structure, space and light, as they played variations upon it. The walks between the mosques vary from five to fifteen minutes each. The itinerary will take at least half a day, but should not be strenuous. It includes good opportunities for restful lunch and coffee stops in historic places. You will refresh yourselves in cool courtyards and enjoy some wonderful views.

It begins at Atik Ali Paşa Camii and Mahmut Paşa Camii, two of the earliest in the city, built by 1496. The next stop is at Sultan Beyazit II Camii, built almost 1000 years after Hagia Sophia, in 1500. This design embodies a central dome and two half domes in the manner of Hagia Sophia, but the space has a very different character. The third stop is Şehzade Camii (1548), designed by the great architect Sinan for Süleyman the Magnificent as a memorial for his son and heir who died young. In Sinan's first large imperial mosque, he demonstrated his structural virtuosity. He covered the interior with a central dome, surrounded by four half domes, making a logical structure and a totally centralised space. Next, in Süleymaniye Camii (1550), Sinan reverted to the theme of Aya Sofya and incorporated only two half domes. But he followed a trend, seen in the two others, of opening up the space. While the nave of Hagia Sophia seems to be hemmed in by piers and arcades that separate it from aisles and galleries, the Ottoman architects have aimed at the creation of a single prayer hall. The tour ends at the small mosque of Rüstem Paşa (1561) down below, close to the Golden Horn. It shows Sinan breaking away from the traditional arrangement of a dome supported on four piers, with two or more half domes, to an octagonal scheme with a dome carried aloft on eight supports. The visit to Rüstem Paşa Camii will offer a treat at the end of the walk, because it is delightfully intimate after the great Süleymaniye Camii, and its sumptuous interior is entirely covered, up to the base of the dome, with İznik tiles.

Route for Itinerary B
Take the tramway to the Çemberlitaş stop (Constantine's Column). On alighting you will see the vast antique column on the north side of the tramway stop. From there can be seen the large Baroque Nuruosmaniye Camii about 200 metres further north (it is visited in Itinerary C.) Pass to the right of it down Vezirhanı Caddesi, which is lined with shops. You will see the gate leading to Mahmut Paşa Camii ahead (13; page 51). The tomb is on the right, just before the mosque. After your visit, return up Vezirhanı Caddesi. When you reach a paved open space, keep to the right side of it and go up a small flight of steps to the Atik Ali Paşa Camii (17; page 56). To continue, turn left out of the porch of the mosque, through an arch and right on Yeniçeriler Caddesi on which the tramway runs. Sultan Beyazit II Camii is on the right, just beyond the Beyazit tramway stop. You will see the tombs first. Turn right into a large open space (18; page 57).

On the east side of the mosque is the traditional Beyazit Tea Garden, and beyond it the Book Bazaar which is a good source of new and used books. The antique market between the two seems to be declining, but may be worth a visit.

If you leave Beyazit II Camii by the portal on the central axis, you will see the imposing gate of the university ahead. You will want to take a street running obliquely to the left of this. First cross the open space diagonally, pass to the right of the Museum of Calligraphic Art (well worth a visit), and go into an underpass to the right of a broad flight of steps. As you emerge, the street curves to the right into Şehzadebaşı Caddesi and you will see

the dome and minaret of Şehzade Camii (22; page 70). Go around the courtyard of Şehzade Camii to the left to find an elegant restaurant in a recently restored *medrese*. You can stop here for coffee, tea or soft drinks as well as meals.

From the gate of Şehzade Camii on Şehzadebaşı Caddesi, turn left along the wall of the precinct and left again at the first corner. The wall of the complex will still be on your left. Some of the buildings of the *külliye* are on your right. When you come to a crossroads with a small mosque on the far side, turn right. 150 metres further on, it is worth making a very short detour through an arch of the Valens Aqueduct to visit the Byzantine Kalenderhane Camii (12; page 49). Return to the same street and continue to the next intersection, where two narrow streets converge from the left at a small fountain. Take the second one, which runs along a high, ancient wall. This is Süleymaniye Caddesi, which will lead you straight to Süleymaniye Camii (23; page 74). An ideal place to eat near the Süleymaniye is the Darüzziyafe Restaurant in the former *imaret* (kitchen) of the *külliye*. Sitting at a table under the arcades of the beautiful court, you can reflect on the sultan's generosity to his subjects while eating traditional Turkish food. For tea or coffee you can go to the adjacent sunken tea garden, the Lale Bahçesi (Tulip Garden). On the southwest side of the Süleymaniye are several small cafes and restaurants.

Leaving Süleymaniye Camii, walk clockwise around it and you will find yourself on a broad terrace overlooking the Golden Horn. Enjoy the spectacular view and continue to the far corner where an enclosed staircase takes you down to the street below. At the foot of the stair, turn right. When you reach a high wall, supporting the terrace of the university above, turn left down the hill on Ismetiye Caddesi. At the third crossroads, turn left on Uzunçarşı Caddesi. You will see a small mosque with a red brick minaret to the right. Continue to descend on this steep narrow street,

teeming with commercial activity. The corner of Rüstem Paşa Camii, with a doorway and staircase, juts out into the street. Climb the stair and you will find yourself on the raised, canopied platform before the mosque (26; page 84). Leave by the staircase at the other end of the terrace. The ten-sided ablutions fountain is off the passage at the foot of these stairs. From here, you will find your way to the waterfront at Eminönü, where you will find various means of transportation. Below Rüstem Paşa Camii at the foot of the staircase, Uzunçarşı Caddesi widens enough for an chestnut tree to spread its branches and shade the tables of a little restaurant that serves a good döner kebab. For a more luxurious lunch, surrounded by İznik tiles, you can go to the nearby Pandeli Restaurant in the Spice Bazaar. It is reached by a staircase just inside the main entrance, on the left.

Itinerary C

Late Classical and Baroque Mosques
See maps opposite and on page 141

This itinerary begins in Eminönü at the Yeni Valide Camii (1597) and proceeds along the tramway route to the vast Sultan Ahmet Camii (1609–16), and on to the Baroque Nuruosmaniye Camii (1748) and Laleli Camii (1759). Since all of them are near tramway stops, very little walking will be necessary. You will see that the design of mosques in the seventeenth and eighteenth centuries was firmly based in classical Ottoman tradition, but that the flamboyance associated with the Baroque asserted itself in the second half of the eighteenth century.

Route for Itinerary C
Begin at Eminönü (see map opposite) where you will have no difficulty in spotting the imposing Yeni Valide Camii (38; page 113). It can be reached by underpass from the tramway, ferry terminal and Galata Bridge. After visiting the mosque, be sure to go around the back

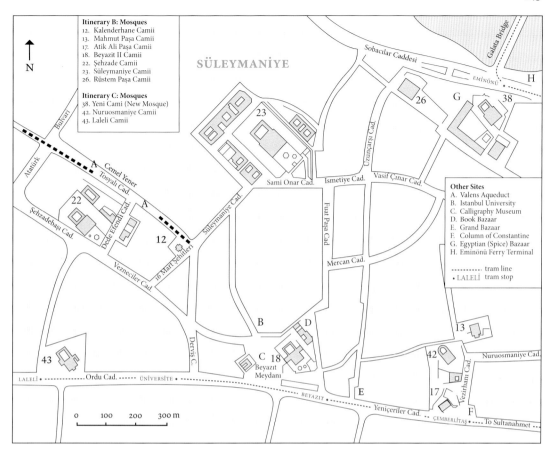

Itinerary B: Mosques
12. Kalenderhane Camii
13. Mahmut Paşa Camii
17. Atik Ali Paşa Camii
18. Beyazıt II Camii
22. Şehzade Camii
23. Süleymaniye Camii
26. Rüstem Paşa Camii

Itinerary C: Mosques
38. Yeni Cami (New Mosque)
42. Nuruosmaniye Camii
43. Laleli Camii

Other Sites
A. Valens Aqueduct
B. Istanbul University
C. Calligraphy Museum
D. Book Bazaar
E. Grand Bazaar
F. Column of Constantine
G. Egyptian (Spice) Bazaar
H. Eminönü Ferry Terminal

------- tram line
• LALELİ tram stop

0   100   200   300 m

to see the very interesting tomb of Turhan Hadice. You should also note, on the southeast side, the entrance and ramp leading up to the *valide sultan's* private rooms and gallery. These were built before the mosque so that Turhan Hadice could watch the building progress. If you wish to have lunch before leaving Eminönü, you could follow the suggestions at the end of Itinerary B.

Cross via the underpass in front of the mosque to the Eminönü tramway stop next to the Galata Bridge. Take the tramway and travel two stops to Sultanahmet (see map on page 141). Cross the tracks and walk through the gardens to Sultan Ahmet Camii (39; page 116; marked as B on the map), whose six minarets proclaim its presence. After your visit, return to the tramway and continue to Çemberlitaş (refer again to the map above). Standing beside Constantine's column, looking north, you will see the obviously Baroque dome of Nuruosmaniye Camii (42; page 124).

Return to the tramway and continue three stops to Laleli for a visit to Laleli Camii (43; page 125). It rises from a high platform close to the stop. Be sure to go into the market underneath and see how the mosque and its *külliye* were supported, both physically and economically.

Itinerary D

The Mosques of Üsküdar
See map on page 144

This itinerary takes you by ferry across the Bosphorus to Üsküdar, where you will find three mosques close to where you land. Two others are reached by a short minibus ride and a few minutes on foot. It could be completed in half a day or extended to occupy a whole, leisurely day. You visit three sixteenth-century mosques by Mimar Sinan, and see how he responds to the sites and varies the arrangement of structure and space. Mihrimah Sultan Camii (1547, otherwise known as İskele Camii) is raised up above the waterfront, with a broad,

sheltering porch, somewhat similarly to Rüstem Paşa Camii. The interior is planned with a dome supported on four piers and three half domes. Atik Valide Sultan Camii (1583), on the slope of the hill above, is Sinan's last and one of his most delightful creations. Its dome, supported on six arches, covers a space flooded with light. The interior, with a long axis at right angles to the *mihrab*, is unique in character. The mosque is entered through a beautiful garden surrounded by shady arcades. Şemsi Ahmet Paşa Camii (1580), Sinan's smallest, is delightfully sited on the waterfront. In addition you can visit the miniscule seventeenth-century Çinili Cami on the hill and Yeni Valide Camii near the ferry. This was built at the end of the Classical period.

Route for Itinerary D
Take the ferry to Üsküdar from Eminönü (just west of the Galata Bridge) or from Kabataş (between mosques 28 and 47) or from Beşiktaş. (Kabataş can be reached from Taksim Square by a new funicular,

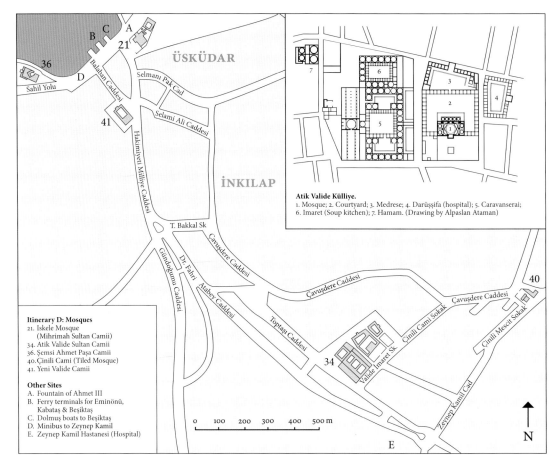

Atik Valide Külliye.
1. Mosque; 2. Courtyard; 3. Medrese; 4. Darüşşifa (hospital); 5. Caravanserai;
6. Imaret (Soup kitchen); 7. Hamam. (Drawing by Alpaslan Ataman)

Itinerary D: Mosques
21. Iskele Mosque
    (Mihrimah Sultan Camii)
34. Atik Valide Sultan Camii
36. Şemsi Ahmet Paşa Camii
40. Çinili Cami (Tiled Mosque)
41. Yeni Valide Camii

Other Sites
A. Fountain of Ahmet III
B. Ferry terminals for Eminönü,
   Kabataş & Beşiktaş
C. Dolmuş boats to Beşiktaş
D. Minibus to Zeynep Kamil
E. Zeynep Kamil Hastanesi (Hospital)

0   100   200   300   400   500 m

N

or Tünel.) These boats run continuously and you will never have to wait long for one. As you approach Üsküdar you will see three of the mosques on the tour. Two are among trees close to the landing place. The third is along the waterfront, to the right. The larger mosques above it on the hill are of lesser interest. The other two mosques on the tour are invisible from the water. Both boats arrive at the same place, right opposite İskele Camii where the tour begins (21; page 67).

From İskele Camii you may wish to take a taxi to Çinili Cami or you can go by minibus. To do this, return to the edge of the water. The dolmuş (minibus) you need stops just opposite the mosque. It will be labelled 'Zeynep Kamil' or 'Z. Kamil' in the window. It will leave as soon as it is full. The minibus will go along the main street, turn left and right and will soon begin to climb a hill. At the top of the hill is a small traffic circle with trees beyond. Alight there and take the level road to the left. This is

Zeynep Kamil Caddesi. (A short detour could be made here, by turning right at the traffic circle instead, to visit the new Sakirin Camii – see page 160.) Walk up Zeynep Kamil Caddesi for about eight minutes. Pass a small mosque on the left. You will see a slightly larger one in a walled enclosure, also on the left. Enter through the gate and visit Çinili Cami (40; page 120).

Leave through the lower gate of the walled precinct of Çinili Cami. Turn left down the main road past a domed *hamam* (Turkish bath). Take the second fork to the left, Çinili Cami Sokak, and walk between apartment buildings until you reach Atik Valide Camii on the right (34; page 104). To return to the ferry terminal, turn right out of the mosque and take the first turning to the right down the hill down Eski Toptaşı Caddesi. Continue in the same direction on Dr Fahri Atabey Caddesi. After the junction continue in the same direction until you see the Yeni Valide Camii, whose large

dome and minaret are visible on the left (see 41; page 122). Then continue to the shore of the Bosphorus.

If you take the last street to the right, Selmanı Pak Caddesi, you will find the elegant Kanaat Lokantası, established in 1933. There is always a huge selection of tempting mezes and meat dishes to choose from. Alternatively you can eat fish on one of several boats moored along the waterfront to the left.

When you reach the waterside promenade, turn left and you will soon see the miniscule Şemsi Ahmet Paşa Camii right on the edge of the Bosphorus (36; page 110). This makes a good end to your walk, because it is particularly attractive in the late afternoon sun.

Itinerary E

The Pilgrimage Site of Eyüp
See map opposite

The short boat trip to Eyüp, at the head of the Golden Horn, makes a pleasant

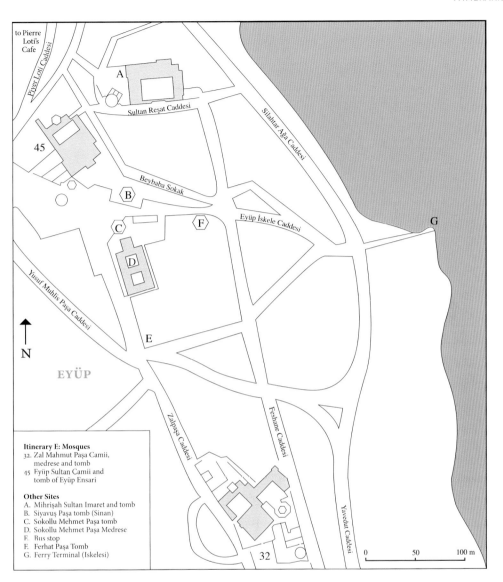

to Pierre Loti's Cafe

Piyer Loti Caddesi

A

Sultan Reşat Caddesi

Silahtar Ağa Caddesi

45

Beybaba Sokak

B

Eyüp İskele Caddesi

C

F

G

D

Yusuf Muhlis Paşa Caddesi

E

N

EYÜP

Zalpaşa Caddesi

Feshane Caddesi

Yavedut Caddesi

Itinerary E: Mosques
32. Zal Mahmut Paşa Camii, medrese and tomb
45 Eyüp Sultan Camii and tomb of Eyüp Ensari

Other Sites
A. Mihrişah Sultan Imaret and tomb
B. Siyavuş Paşa tomb (Sinan)
C. Sokollu Mehmet Paşa tomb
D. Sokollu Mehmet Paşa Medrese
E. Bus stop
F. Ferhat Paşa Tomb
G. Ferry Terminal (Iskelesi)

32

0   50   100 m

change from the intensity of Istanbul. As the reputed burial place of Eyüp al Ensari, the friend and standard bearer of Muhammad, it is regarded as the third most important pilgrimage site of Islam. I would recommend going there on a Sunday when it is crowded with pilgrims. It is a joyful place where you may see young boys, in special costumes, brought by their parents to celebrate their circumcision, and brides in their white wedding dresses with soberly suited grooms, who have come to ask for a blessing after their weddings. You will see two important mosques, the tomb of Eyüp al Ensari, a Baroque *külliye*, and countless tombs of grandees who

wanted to be laid to rest in good company. You can climb up through the cemetery, where thousands more are buried, to the Pierre Loti Café (or take the cable car from the shore, if you prefer). There is a superb view of the Golden Horn, as far as the Galata Tower and Topkapı Palace. On the way back on the boat, you could stop at Kasımpaşa on the north bank of the Golden Horn and visit Piyale Paşa Camii almost two kilometres north.

Route for Itinerary E
You will need to plan this trip ahead because there is only one boat an hour from Eminönü. The schedule is posted at all ferry terminals. The *iskele* for the

boats to Eyüp is quite hard to find. From Galata Bridge, walk west along the Golden Horn past a ferry dock announcing several destinations. Continue through the bus station, turn left past small ticket booths and sharp right around a car park, and go down a path to the right. This brings you to the Eminönü Haliç *iskelesi*.

Arriving at Eyüp you will see the dome and two minarets of Eyüp Sultan Camii to the right and Zal Mahmut Paşa Camii to the left before you land. These will help to orient you. Walk up Eyüp İskele Caddesi past two large tombs opposite each other. These are the resting places of Sokollu Mehmet Paşa on the left and Siyavuş Paşa on the right, both by Sinan.

Alternatively, you can take bus 99A from the bus station just mentioned. The bus goes along the shore, which is lined with parks. Immediately after a double curve in the road, leading away from the water, get off at a stop marked Zalpaşa. Take the road to the right and you will see Eyüp Sultan Camii ahead.

Eyüp Sultan Camii is entered through two gates from the plaza with the fountain (45; page 128). Just south of the fountain is the Mihmandar Lokantası where you can eat outside under coloured umbrellas. There are also other cafés and restaurants nearby.

To reach Zal Mahmut Paşa Camii, only 325 metres away, go south on a mainly pedestrian street towards Yusuf Muhlis Paşa Caddesi, on which the buses run. Cross this street into Zalpaşa Caddesi; walk past a small mosque on the left. Zal Mahmut Paşa Camii, recognisable by its polychrome walls of brick and stone, will be on your left (32; page 102).

Before leaving Eyüp, it is worth looking at the Baroque *imaret* and tomb of Mihrişah Sultan just east of Eyüp Sultan Camii, as well as some of the tombs nearby. To reach the Pierre Loti Café or to enjoy the views from the hillside, go to the north end of the plaza with the fountain, turn right along a cobbled street and in about 50 metres, fork left up some steps to a footpath through the cemetery. A ten-minute walk will take you to the café. Alternatively, a cable car runs from the Golden Horn shore.

If you decide to visit Piyale Paşa Camii (31; page 101) on the way back, take the boat from the Eyüp *iskelesi* as far as Kasımpaşa on the left bank. This was the site of the busiest naval arsenal in the world at the height of Ottoman naval power. Turn right along the shore until you come to Bahriye Caddesi. Turn left up the hill, about one kilometre, then turn left on Dolapdere Caddesi, a main road that turns into Piyale Paşa Bulvarı. Continue for another kilometre and you will

see a cemetery on a slope to the right, and the mosque set back on the left. Buses run from Bahriye Caddesi up Piyale Paşa Bulvarı, but a taxi would be easier.

Itinerary F

Fatih, Selim and Along the Landwalls
See map opposite

This walk includes several important mosques to the northwest and west of the Süleymaniye district. It begins with the *külliye* of Mehmet I (known as Fatih, meaning Conqueror). The mosque seen here today is an eighteenth-century replacement of Fatih's mosque which was destroyed in an earthquake. It is followed by the mosque built by Süleyman for his father, Selim the Grim, and three later mosques by Sinan. As you return you can visit Sinan's first commission: Haseki Camii and *külliye*. The distances between the first four mosques are not more than about fifteen minutes. The next stretch is the longer and you will certainly need a taxi or a bus after that.

Route for Itinerary F
Begin at Fatih Camii (14 and 44; pages 53 and 126) on Macar Kardeşler Caddesi. This can be reached by a bus from Taksim or from Beşiktaş via Eminönü. From the Sultanahmet district you will need to change buses at the intersection between Atatürk Bulvarı and Macar Kardeşler Caddesi. Fatih Camii cannot be seen from the road, but you will see the high walls of the *külliye* when you arrive. After your visit, walk northwest along the terrace on the side of the mosque nearest to the Golden Horn and leave the precinct through a gate leading into Darüşşafaka Caddesi, which is very lively on market days. You will pass five small streets on the right. Ignore these and after about 400 metres you will come to a major intersection, beyond which are two schools. Turn right here onto Yavuz Selim Caddesi.

As soon as you turn, you will see the dome and minaret of Sultan Selim Camii

(19; page 60). As you go towards it you will notice a large rectangular depression in the ground; this is the remains of a Byzantine reservoir. Do not miss the tomb, with early İznik tiles or the view of the Golden Horn from the terrace. Leave Sultan Selim Camii by Yavuz Selim Caddesi, the road by which you came. Pass the intersection where you turned before and continue 150 metres to the top of a rise. Take the second turning on the right as the road goes downhill again. This is Fatih Nişancı Caddesi. Nişancı Mehmet Paşa Camii will be on the left in about 200 metres (37; page 111). After visiting the mosque, continue on the same street, which curves gently left and right for about 500 metres and ends in a broad flight of steps. Climb these and you will be on Fevzi Paşa Caddesi, a major highway. The high dome of the Mihrimah Sultan Camii (27; page 91) will soon come into view. Continue another 500 metres to Edirnekapı (Edirne Gate) in the Theodosian Walls. The local restaurants here, which serve döner kebabs and various ready-cooked foods at outdoor tables, would be your best bet for lunch on this walk.

To reach the next mosque, take the road that leads south along the inside of the Theodosian walls towards Topkapı, but stop short of it. After crossing a major road that breaches the wall (Adnan Menderes Caddesi) continue, keeping close to the wall until you come to an open space with a kiosk among trees and a taxi stand beside a small gate in the wall. Turn left here and you will find Kara Ahmet Paşa Camii on the left in 200 metres (24; page 82). Go out of the gate of the mosque, cross the road, and, leaving the small traffic circle on your right, continue down Topkapı Caddesi past hotels and shops. This leads to Millet Caddesi and the Pazartekke tramway stop. You can take the tramway along Millet Caddesi to Haseki (or, if you don't want to stop for a mosque that is often closed between prayer times, continue to the Yusufpaşa

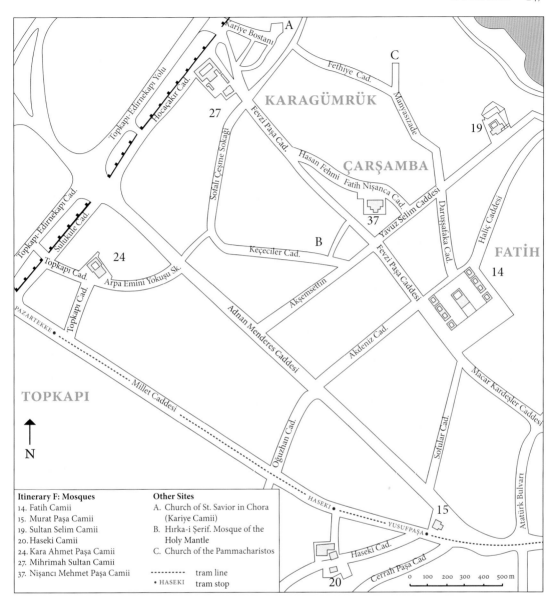

Itinerary F: Mosques
14. Fatih Camii
15. Murat Paşa Camii
19. Sultan Selim Camii
20. Haseki Camii
24. Kara Ahmet Paşa Camii
27. Mihrimah Sultan Camii
37. Nişancı Mehmet Paşa Camii

Other Sites
A. Church of St. Savior in Chora (Kariye Camii)
B. Hırka-i Şerif. Mosque of the Holy Mantle
C. Church of the Pammacharistos

---------- tram line
• HASEKI tram stop

0 100 200 300 400 500 m

stop). At the Haseki stop, cross to the south side of the street, turn right and almost immediately left. At the top of a gentle slope, you will see the impressive buildings of the Bayrampaşa *külliye*, recognisable by its four colossal chimneys to the right. The hospital of the Haseki *külliye* is straight ahead. Keep to the left of this and follow the high wall towards a large dome; turn right on Haseki Caddesi and you will see the twin domes of the Haseki Camii on the left (20; page 66). After visiting the mosque turn right down Haseki Caddesi which will take you back to Millet Caddesi. Cross it to

the Murat Paşa Camii (15; page 54). The Tramway will take you back to Sultanahmet or Eminönü.

Itinerary G

Beyoğlu and the Bosphorus Shore
See map on page 138–39

This itinerary begins with the two late mosques by Sinan, followed by four nineteenth-century mosques. The distances are fairly long on busy streets, so you might want to do some stretches by bus or taxi. The route begins with the second mosque built by Sinan for

Sokollu Mehmet Paşa, now isolated beside the Atatürk Bridge, and Kılıç Ali Paşa Camii. The first of these is a miniature version of Selimiye Camii in Edirne; the second returns to the theme of Hagia Sophia. The four later mosques show how, in the nineteenth century, the Ottomans embraced European styles.

The tramway now runs over Galata Bridge to Kabataş. If you want a shorter walk, you may take the tram to Tophane and begin at the Kılıç Ali Paşa Camii.

Route for Itinerary G
Begin at the northern end of Atatürk

Bridge, where Sokollu Mehmet Paşa Camii stands between the bridge and the shore (33; page 103). After visiting it you can walk along Tershane Caddesi, a busy commercial street, to the northern end of Galata Bridge. Here you can either take the tramway from Karaköy stop or you can continue walking. If you take the tram, travel one stop and get off at Tophane.

If you prefer to walk, cross the main road going north by the underpass and walk down to the shore. Go north beside the water, past the Karaköy Ferry Terminal, and follow Kemankeş Caddesi, which is separated from the shore by buildings connected to maritime commerce. In about 500 metres it will curve to the left into Tophane İskelesi Caddesi. You will see the elegant Tophane Fountain at the end of the street and, on the slope above, the Tophane (cannon foundry) which gave the district its name. In front of you is the tramway stop.

To the left of the fountain is Kılıç Ali Paşa Camii (35; page 108). 150 metres further north is Nusretiye Camii (46; page 132). Istanbul Modern, the city's new modern art museum, is situated

behind the mosque on the Bosphorus shore. It has a fine riverside restaurant.

The next stretch is rather longer, about 1.5 kilometres, but you can walk part of the way through parks along the shore, or you can take the tramway two more stops, getting out at the end of the line at Kabataş.

After the Kabataş Ferry Terminal you will come to Dolmabahçe Camii (47; page 135). From there you can take a bus to Beşiktaş. Sinan Paşa Camii is opposite the ferry terminal (25; page 83). From Beşiktaş Hamidiye Camii at Yıldız Palace is 750 metres inland (49; page 137). To reach it, turn up Barbaros Bulvarı, the major highway going uphill to the left, or to escape the traffic walk through the park on the north side of it. The mosque stands at the end of the park near the entrances to Yıldız Technical University and Yıldız Palace. Return to Beşiktaş, cross the main road and take a bus or taxi to Ortaköy. Mecidiye Camii is right on the waterfront in this popular village (48; page 136). Ortaköy is well known for its restaurants and cafés and you will find a wide range of places to choose from.

Itinerary H

Bursa – Early Mosques in the First Capital
See map below

This walk starts in the Hisar, the former Byzantine citadel which was captured, after a long siege, by Orhan in 1326. His father Osman, founder of the Ottoman dynasty, was too weak to join him, but died knowing of the victory. The high, naturally defensible place has been transformed by modern building, but still conveys its fortress-like quality. Nothing remains of Orhan's wooden palace, while the few old houses that survive date from later centuries, but using your imagination you will be able to visualise the ancient walls overlooking the site of today's vast city. From a string of parks along the southern edge of the fortress, you can look down on the *külliyes* established by Orhan, his son and grandson. Along the itinerary you will appreciate the eye for topography of these sultans. Although you will gradually descend, you will find each of the mosques standing in a commanding position as the nucleus of a district. You will experience two types of mosque:

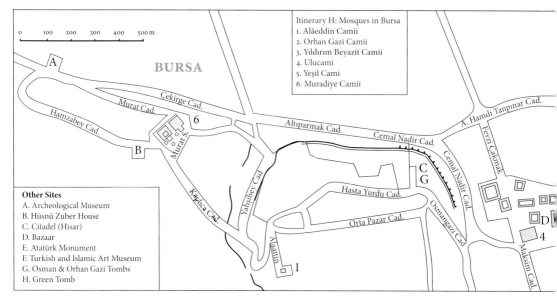

Itinerary H: Mosques in Bursa
1. Alâeddin Camii
2. Orhan Gazi Camii
3. Yıldırım Beyazit Camii
4. Ulucami
5. Yeşil Cami
6. Muradiye Camii

BURSA

Other Sites
A. Archeological Museum
B. Hüsnü Zuber House
C. Citadel (Hisar)
D. Bazaar
E. Atatürk Monument
F. Turkish and Islamic Art Museum
G. Osman & Orhan Gazi Tombs
H. Green Tomb

the so-called "Bursa type" with three *eyvans* opening off a covered court and the Ulucami, which inherits the old Islamic tradition of mosques that spread horizontally without a dominant dome. You will also see the fascinating ways in which the architects make the transition from the square of the walls to the circle of the dome. None of the walks between sites is more than fifteen minutes, except the last one from Yıldırım Beyazit Camii to Muradiye Camii, which calls for a bus or taxi.

Route for itinerary H
From the western end of Atatürk Caddesi, the remains of the Hisar walls are visible on the left. Go up Osmangazi Caddesi, which climbs beside them. When the road curves to the left, you will see an ornate gateway to the right and the tombs of Osman and Orhan. Since they were rebuilt after an earthquake in 1855, they are of little architectural interest. But, standing beside them, you can imagine the momentous day when Orhan brought his father's body to this high vantage point for burial. After visiting the tombs, go to the right-hand side of the small park and

down some steps. From here you will get a good view of the many domes of the *hans* in the market area and, to their right, the domes and minarets of Ulucami. Beyond, a little to the left, you may be able to make out the distant Yeşil Cami and tomb, and, further still to the left, Yıldırım Beyazit Camii in its *külliye*. At the end of the garden around the tombs is a six-storied clocktower. From here you can return to Atatürk Boulevard, but if you want to see the first mosque of Bursa (open only at prayer times), continue on Osmangazi Caddesi, past a hospital and a small mosque on an island in the middle of the road. After this, the road will curve to the left and begin to go downhill. From a little tea garden on the right you will get a good view of the Muradiye *külliye*. Alaattin Camii Caddesi leads to the left before the main road plunges steeply downhill. Take this narrow street, which winds between old houses, giving you a taste of the medieval layout of the Hisar. It leads directly to Alâeddin Camii (1; page 22). You can make your way back by turning left after it and weaving through the narrow streets. The most direct way, Orta Pazar Caddesi,

is uninteresting. If you follow the map and pick your way eastwards through the smaller streets, you will find your way to the town centre again.

When you reach Atatürk Boulevard, cross to the north side by an underpass and walk past the large, many-domed Ulucami. Beyond it is a public garden, with the twin domes of Orhan Gazi Camii visible at the far end (2; page 23). Close to this mosque, beside the entrance, the underpass crossing the boulevard is the Tourist Information Office where a good map and guide are available. After looking at this mosque, return to visit the Ulucami (4; page 26). Then continue eastwards along Atatürk Caddesi. There are several small restaurants in the pleasant courtyards of the *hans* and in the surrounding markets. Alternatively, if you go straight on down a pedestrian street, after passing the Atatürk statue, instead of taking the right fork you could try the Iskender Restaurant on the left and rejoin the route by keeping right.

At the equestrian statue of Atatürk, take the right fork (still Atatürk Boulevard), cross a ravine with a small river running through it and then take the left fork, Yeşil Caddesi. The green tiled wall of the Yeşil Türbe will appear ahead, and to its left the Yeşil Cami (5; page 30). After your visit, go a few steps back to the west from the area between the mosque and the tomb and turn right, down Yeşil Sokak. Follow this street past some old houses and you will see a large highway ahead. You need to take the parallel street to its right. Ignore the sign to Yıldırım; stay on the raised sidewalk until you can cross Beyazit Caddesi to Kurtuluş Caddesi. Walk along it, over a crossroads with traffic lights and, after passing three small streets close together, take the fourth turning on the right. This is Yıldırım Camii Sokak; it leads uphill to Yıldırım Beyazit Camii (3; page 24). The mosque stands on a mound, and beneath it are the buildings of the *külliye* as well as Beyazit's tomb.

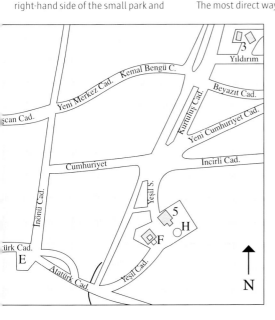

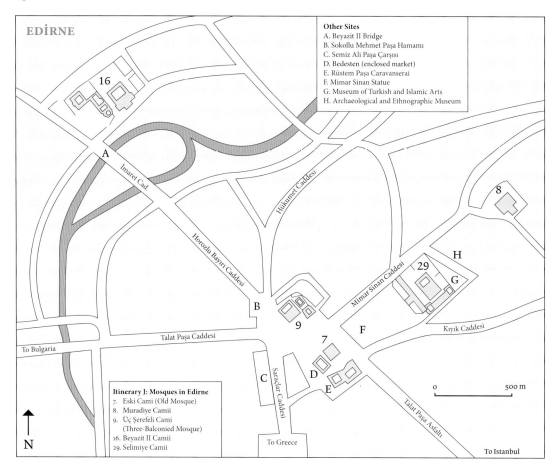

EDİRNE

Other Sites
A. Beyazit II Bridge
B. Sokollu Mehmet Paşa Hamamı
C. Semiz Ali Paşa Çarşısı
D. Bedesten (enclosed market)
E. Rüstem Paşa Caravanserai
F. Mimar Sinan Statue
G. Museum of Turkish and Islamic Arts
H. Archaeological and Ethnographic Museum

Imaret Cad.
Hükümet Caddesi
Horozlu Bayırı Caddesi
Mimar Sinan Caddesi
Talat Paşa Caddesi
To Bulgaria
Kıyık Caddesi
Saraçlar Caddesi
Talat Paşa Asfaltı
To Greece
To Istanbul

0   500 m

N

Itinerary J: Mosques in Edirne
7. Eski Cami (Old Mosque)
8. Muradiye Camii
9. Üç Şerefeli Cami
    (Three-Balconied Mosque)
16. Beyazit II Camii
29. Selimiye Camii

To visit Muradiye Camii (6; page 34), you need to return to the west side of the town centre. A taxi would be the easiest way, but perhaps you can find a bus on the main road that goes to the Muradiye district. Either vehicle will go a long way round to follow a one-way system. Muradiye Camii can be approached either from Kaplıca Caddesi or Murat Caddesi. It is worth going into several of the tombs as well as the mosque if a guide is available to open them.

Itinerary J

Edirne – Evolving Tradition
See map above

The three major mosques of Edirne are all close together in the centre of the city, and the openness of the townscape makes it easy to find them. Two others can be reached on foot in 15 and 25 minutes, or by taxi.

Route for Itinerary J
You can orient yourself if you stand by the bronze statue of Sinan at the foot of the park that slopes up towards the monumental Selimiye Camii. Nearby, to the southeast, you will see Eski Cami (1403) with its two sturdy minarets and nine small domes rising above the plain walls (7; page 36). To the northwest, less than a five-minute walk away, stands the more complex Üç Şerefeli Cami (1438) with four minarets and one dome rising above the others (9; page 38). The crowning glory of Edirne, Selimiye Camii (1568), with its single high dome and four soaring minarets, dominates the scene (29; page 93). I suggest that you experience the dramatic evolution of Ottoman architecture by looking at them in the order in which they were built. You can also get an idea of the related buildings. Close to the Eski Cami you will find the many domed *bedestan* and the Caravanserai, now a hotel. Opposite the Üç Şerefeli

Cami is the Hamam of Sokollu Mehmet Paşa, designed by Sinan and still in use. The complex around Selimiye Camii is vast, stretching from the Kavaflar Arasta (covered bazaar) on the southwest side to the *medrese* in the north corner, now housing the Museum of Turkish and Islamic arts. I suggest that you enter the Selimiye complex through the small gate on Mimar Sinan Caddesi and experience the sequence described on page 95.

To walk to Muradiye Camii go one kilometre northeast, on Mimar Sinan Caddesi (8; page 37). You will need to plan your visit carefully because it is open only at prayer times. The Beyazit complex (16; page 55), about 1.5 kilometres from the centre, is reached by turning left up Horozlu Bayır Caddesi just north of the Sokollu Mehmet Paşa Hamamı. You will soon come to the edge of the city and pass over one of the historic bridges that cross the river Tunca. The mosque and its huge *külliye* are immediately visible.

Blair, Sheila S., *Islamic Calligraphy* (Edinburgh University Press, 2006). This exquisite book offers the most complete explanation of Islamic calligraphy for the layman, and shows its significance with the help of many colour illustrations.

Carswell, John, *Iznik Pottery* (British Museum Press, 1998). A good introduction to the subject with helpful coverage of the İznik tiles in Ottoman mosques.

Denny, Walter, *The Artistry of Ottoman Ceramics* (Thames and Hudson, London, 2005). This book contains beautiful colour photographs of İznik ceramics, many of them from mosques in Istanbul.

Derman, M. Uğur, *Letters in Gold* (The Metropolitan Museum of Art, 1998). This is the catalogue of an exhibition of Ottoman calligraphy. Although the illustrations do not include architectural inscriptions, the book offers an excellent introduction to the art.

Finkel, Caroline, *Osman's Dream* (John Murray, London, 2005). This history of the Ottoman Empire, with a focus on military history, has received critical acclaim.

Goodwin, Godfrey, *A History of Ottoman Architecture* (Thames and Hudson, 2003). This is the most comprehensive book on Ottoman architecture with many plans, sections and photographs. Although written in a somewhat confusing manner, it is an essential resource for further study. It covers the whole of Turkey.

Günay, Reha, *Sinan: the Architect and his Works* (Milet Publishing Limited, 2000). The many beautiful colour photographs by the author and the effective organization make this an excellent introduction to Sinan.

Kuran, Aptullah, *The Mosque in Early Ottoman Architecture* (University of Chicago Press, 1968). This is by far the best book on Ottoman architecture before the age of Sinan. The many drawings, some of which are reproduced in this book by kind permission of the author, are extremely helpful.

Kuran, Aptullah, *Sinan: The Grand Old Master of Ottoman Architecture* (ADA Press, Istanbul, and Institute of Turkish Studies, Washington D.C., 1987). This is a substantial work on Sinan by a leading scholar. Well written, and illustrated with many drawings and photographs.

Necipoğlu, Gülru, *The Age of Sinan: Architectural Culture in the Ottoman Empire 1539–1588* (Reaktion Books, London, and Princeton University Press, 2005). This is the most authoritative work on Sinan, based on the latest research. It is well illustrated with many plans and three-dimensional drawings as well as photographs.

The Rough Guide to Turkish: A Dictionary Phrasebook (Penguin Books, 2000). By far the best phrasebook. It includes a clear introduction to Turkish grammar and an intelligent selection of useful phrases in dictionary form.

GLOSSARY OF TURKISH AND ARABIC TERMS

To help explain Turkish terms used in the text (and to avoid lengthy explanation and repetition), italics have been used throughout this book to indicate the words that are defined in this Glossary. In addition, some words in this Glossary do not appear in the book, but you might find it useful to be familiar with them. Overleaf you will find a separate glossary of English architectural terms.

Ağa

A term of respect; chief; master; a title given to chief architects (e.g. Mehmet Ağa).

Arasta

A market, sometimes associated with a mosque, often covered by vaults.

Avlu

The courtyard of a mosque.

Bedesten

An enclosed market for the sale of valuable goods.

Bimarhane

A hospital, usually in the *külliye* of a mosque.

Cami / Camii

A mosque. A mosque where sermons are preached at noon on Fridays. The possessive form, "Camii" is used when it follows a name rather than an adjective. (e.g. Süleymaniye Camii means Suleyman's mosque, and Eski Cami means old mosque.)

Çeşme

A drinking fountain.

Dar-ül- hadis

College of religious law.

Dar-ül-kurra

House for readers of the *Qur'an*.

Darüşşifa

A hospital.

Dershane

A classroom in a *medrese*.

Dervish

A member of a mystical order, somewhat like a monk.

Devşirme

The system by which carefully selected non-Muslims were recruited to serve in the Janissary corps. The most promising of them were given a superior education, and offered the opportunity to rise to high positions, such as grand vizier, chief admiral of the Ottoman fleet or chief architect.

Eyvan

A large recess opening off a court or from the central space of a mosque in Seljuk or early Ottoman architecture.

Hamam

A Turkish bath, often part of a *külliye*, for thorough ablutions before prayer.

Han

An inn providing accommodation for travellers.

Hünkâr mahfili

Sultan's lodge in a mosque, usually raised up for privacy and protection.

Imam

Religious leader in Islam.

Imaret

A kitchen serving food to the staff of a mosque, students and the poor.

Kadın

Woman; also concubine.

Külliye

A group of educational and charitable buildings associated with a mosque.

Medrese

A religious school, usually in the *külliye* of a mosque.

Mekteb

A school for young boys.

Mescit

A small mosque without a *minber*, not used for Friday prayers.

Meydan

A public open space or square.

Mihrab

A niche in the *qibla* wall of a mosque, to which prayers are directed. It is often covered with a *muqarnas* vault. See page 15.

Mimar
Architect or master builder
(e.g. Mimar Sinan).

Minber
A tall pulpit, approached by a
flight of steps, from which the
Friday sermon is preached in
a mosque. It is usually covered
with a conical canopy. See
page 15.

Molla
Senior member of the *Ulema*.

Müezzin
The official of a mosque who gives
the call to prayer.

Müezzin mahfili
Raised platform from which the
müezzin chants prayers.

Muqarnas
A 'stalactite' vault or surface of a
pendentive or capital. See page 19.
(Arabic; **Mukarnes** in Turkish)

Nişancı
Secretary of the Imperial council.

Paşa
An Ottoman general or high official.

Qibla
The direction of Mecca. The *mihrab*
is always on the *qibla* wall.

Qur'an
The sacred book of Islam. The
revelations of God to the Prophet
Muhammad.

Revak
Arcaded walk on the side(s) of a
court. For the porch of the mosque,
see *son cemaat yeri*.

Şadırvan
A fountain for ablutions before
prayer, found at every mosque.

Saray
Palace.

Sebil
A fountain from which cups
of water are given by an
attendant.

Şerefe
Balcony on the shaft of a minaret.

Şeriat
Muslim religious law.

Şifahane
Hospital.

Son cemaat yeri
The porch of a mosque, often with a
raised platform for latecomers.

Tabhane
Hospice.

Tanzimat
Reforms put in place by Sultan
Abdülmecid (1839–61).

Tekke
A lodge for dervishes.

Tımarhane
An asylum for the mentally ill.

Türbe
A tomb.

Ulema
Scholars of Islamic law.

Valide sultan
Mother of the sultan, who could
have enormous political power.

Vakıf
A pious foundation. Wealthy people
satisfied their obligation to charity
(one of the five pillars of Islam) by
founding or donating to *vakıfs*. By
doing so they avoided taxes.

Vezir (vizier)
A minister of state in the Ottoman
court

GLOSSARY OF ENGLISH ARCHITECTURAL TERMS

Apse

A semi-circular space, usually at the east end of an Early Christian or Byzantine church.

Arch

A curved structure that spans an opening in a wall, or between two columns. It is constructed with wedge-shaped stones known as **voussoirs**. The Romans used only round arches, but in Islamic architecture arches were often slightly pointed. **Ogee arches** also appeared.

Arcade

A row of arches supported on columns or piers. The courtyards of mosques are almost always surrounded by arcades. The vaulted or domed walk behind the arches is also referred to as an arcade.

Buttress

A masonry structure built against a wall, and bonded to it, to resist the pressure of a dome or a vault.

Capital

The spreading upper part of a **column** that makes the transition from the shaft of the column to the beams or arches it supports. The type of capital on a column is generally the key to its style and character. The capitals of the Greek and Roman Doric, Ionic and Corinthian orders were signifiers of three styles. Byzantine capitals were more open to variation by the craftsmen. In Ottoman architecture two types prevail, one based on the *muqarnas*, the other employs the same geometry as the **Turkish band of triangles**. In the Baroque era, modified versions of Ionic capitals were sometimes used.

Column

A slender cylindrical support with a **capital**. Greek and Roman columns were generally fluted (grooved), while Ottoman columns were smooth. The richly coloured marble or porphyry shafts of Roman columns were highly prized and

these were often reused with new capitals in Ottoman mosques.

Conch

A semi-circular enclosure covered with a half dome. See also Exedra.

Dome

A convex masonry structure, usually hemispherical, covering a space. While **vaults** were the normal means of covering medieval churches, Ottoman builders almost always built domes. Domes are far more durable than wooden roofs and have often survived earthquakes.

Drum

The cylindrical structure on which a dome stands. In Ottoman architecture, for sound structural reasons, the drums of domes often lean slightly inwards. Since there are many windows in them, the drums of most Ottoman domes are heavily buttressed.

Exedra

A semi-circular recess similar to the apse of a church or a large niche, usually covered with a half dome. In Byzantine churches exedrae (note plural form) were sometimes opened up through arches to the aisles or galleries behind. Domed exedrae are sometimes referred to as conches.

Iconostasis

A screen between the nave and apse of a Byzantine church, concealing the altar. Often hung with icons.

Lunette

The area between the lintel over a door or window and the arch above. This was often filled with tiled decoration or calligraphy.

Narthex

Portico at the west end of a basilica; a rectangular entrance hall between the porch and the nave of a church.

Oculus

A circular opening in the crown of a dome, as in the Pantheon.

Ogee arch

An arch with an S-curved line on

either side of it, curving up to a central point.

Pendentive

A structural device making the transition from rectangular walls to the circle of a dome. It takes the form of a convex triangle of masonry. When the dome stands on six or eight supports, the form of the pendentive is modified. In Ottoman architecture the surfaces of the pendentives are sometimes ornamented with *muqarnas;* see page 22.

Pier

A massive column, sometimes square in section, designed to take a major load, for example a section of a dome. Four huge piers support the dome of Süleymaniye Camii.

Revetment

A facing, usually of stone, to protect a wall.

Soffit

The surface under the eaves of a roof, or under an arch or vault.

Squinch

An alternative to **pendentives** for making the transition from a square structure to the circular base of a dome. It consists of an arch spanning across a corner. The spaces behind squinches may be filled with *muqarnas*, scalloped conches, or small half domes; see also page 22.

Tympanum

The semi-circular area of wall beneath an arch. The wall penetrated by windows under a large arch supporting a dome.

Turkish band of triangles

An ingenious means of making the transition from rectangular walls to the circle of a dome, by means of a series of three-dimensional triangular forms. This alternative to **pendentives** was used in early Ottoman mosques, particularly in Bursa; see also page 22.

Voussoir

A wedge-shaped stone in an arch. In Ottoman architecture alternate voussoirs are often of different coloured stone or brick, to create a polychrome effect.

Vault

An arched masonry structure covering a space. In Ottoman architecture domes were preferred to vaults. While, in Medieval Europe, the aisles of churches were usually vaulted, Ottoman architects covered similar spaces with a series of small domes.

Weight tower

A structural device, serving the same purpose as a pinnacle in Gothic architecture, to resist the outward thrust of a dome or a **vault**. Weight towers stand directly over the structure supporting a dome, so that their massive weight, pulled downwards by gravity, counteracts the diagonal thrust of the dome. Weight towers can often be seen above the roof of a mosque. See page 71.

INDEX

Note: A page number in roman type indicates a term that appears in the main text and may also appear in the captions on the same page; whereas one in *italics* refers to the captions only. A number in **bold** refers to the itineraries at the end of the book. The glossaries and chronological table are not indexed.

In the alphabetical ordering, no distinction is made between the letter 'ş' and 's'; and similarly between 'ü' and 'u'.

First published in 2010 in Turkey by
Scala Yayıncılık
Ankara Cad. No. 107
Hoşağası Han, Dük. 78
Cağaloğlu, Istanbul, Turkey

First published in 2010 in the rest of the
world by
Scala Publishers Ltd
Northburgh House
10 Northburgh Street
London EC1V OAT
www.scalapublishers.com

Series Editor: Brian Johnson
Project Editors: Miranda Harrison, Oliver
Craske, Jessica Hodge
Copy editor: Howard Watson
Design: Anikst Design (Misha Anikst and
James Warner)
Architectural drawings by Anikst Design
unless indicated otherwise

ISBN (Turkey): 978-605-88606-0-5

ISBN (rest of the world): 978-1-85759-307-5

Front cover: Sultan Ahmet Camii (the
Blue Mosque), viewed from the
westernmost of its six minarets, with
Istanbul's Asian shore visible in the back-
ground across the Sea of Marmara.
Robert Harding Picture Library Ltd/Alamy

Back cover: Yıldırım Beyazit Camii in
Bursa: a view of the principal prayer hall,
with *mihrab* and *minber. Erdal Yazıcı*
Page 2: Sokollu Mehmet Paşa Camii: interior with tiled *minber* (pulpit) in foreground. *Erdal Yazıcı*

Interior Photographic Credits
Erdal Yazıcı: 2, 21, 24, 27, 29R, 31, 34–5,
40, 42, 44–8, 56, 57, 60–1, 67–71, 74, 75,
77, 82, 88–90, 91R, 93, 100R, 106–7, 109,
111–15, 117T, 118–127, 130–1, 133,
135–7.
Henry Matthews: 13–20, 23, 28–9, 32,
36, 39, 50, 51, 55, 58, 62–5, 72, 73, 79,
80, 83–7, 91L, 92, 94–7, 100T, 102–5,
108, 110, 117B, 128, 129, 132, 134.
Reha Günay: 66, 76, 99.

This book is also available in a Turkish
edition, *Istanbul'un Camileri* by Henry
Matthews (edited by Dr M. Numan
Malkoç).

Printed in Turkey

10 9 8 7 6 5 4 3 2 1

Addendum:
A modern mosque in Istanbul

ŞAKİRİN CAMİİ (Itinerary D)
Üsküdar 2008–10

The Şakirin Camii in Üsküdar is
the best known truly modern
mosque in Istanbul. It is dedicated
to the memory of Ibrahim and
Semiha Şakir by their children. The
interior designer Zeynep Fadıllıoğlu
has the distinction of being the first
woman to design a mosque. The
architect is Hüsrev Tayla. The interi-
or is suffused with light subtly
filtered through etched glass, with
abstract patterns in gold leaf, and
screened by decorative metalwork.
Glass drops overhead , shimmering
below the red ceiling, were inspired
by the idea that Allah's light should
shine on you like rain. In the courtyard is a fountain by the British
sculptor William Pye in the form of a
pefect sphere with water running
over its polished surface. This
mosque is easy to visit.

Route
Follow itinerary D on pages 143–144
and when you go to the top of the
hill to visit the Çinili Cami, turn right
at the traffic circle at Zeynep Kamil.
In less than five minutes you will see
the minarets.